Green Stamps to Hot Pants

Also by Genny Zak Kieley

Heart and Hard Work:
Memories of "Nordeast" Minneapolis

Pride and Tradition:
More Memories of Northeast Minneapolis

Roots and Ties:
A Scrapbook of Northeast Minneapolis

For more information visit
gennykieleybooks.com

GREEN STAMPS TO HOT PANTS

Growing Up in the 50s and 60s

Genny Zak Kieley

NODIN PRESS

Fourteenth printing, September 2013

Design and Layout: John Toren
"Photographic Tour Down Memory Lane" layout: Genny Kieley
Collage photos: Melanie Kieley

Library of Congress Control Number: 2008939926

ISBN 978-1-932472-73-8

Nodin Press, LLC
5114 Cedar Lake Road
Minneapolis, MN
55416

TO ANDY

For living a life of passion
For using your talents
For helping others to recognize theirs
For the grin on your face
For opening your heart to so many
For never giving up
For being a mentor to Anthony and DJ
And so many others
For living your dreams
For believing and sharing in mine
For changing lives
Almost from the day you were born
I have not forgotten you
And will continue to write your story
I am a part of you
And you of me
At the end of my days
I will walk toward the bridge of light
And meet you there

I will love you always, Mom

Acknowledgements

To my Writing Group on Wednesday nights that have continued to be supportive of me after nearly twenty years together. Thanks for your continued encouragement and blessings: Judy, Lyn, Ross, Judd, Jack, Janet, Sue, Laura and Larry. I love you all and couldn't do it without you. To my other day group that is a spin off of Maureen LaJoy's writing classes: Linda, Kim, Al, Joanne, Vern, Stephanie and Bernie. My hope is that all of your own writing dreams will come true.

Thanks to my two dear friends, LuAnn Golen and Joannie Moses for believing in my project even in the beginning stages. Also for sharing my love of looking back at the 50s and 60s. They helped to collect memorabilia, called me up with ideas, took photos and even arranged them. You have been a blessing to me.

To those who shared their memories and photos with me: Pam Albinson, Frank Dattalo, Betty Dymanyk, Linda Herkenhoff, Betty Kieley, Doug Kieley, Joannie Moses, Nancy O'Dette, Linda Petroske and Richard Worthing—my gracious thanks. Your interesting views and support made the book much more fun and interesting.

To Jack Kabrud of the Hennepin History Center, who is always there sharing his memories. Thank you for your love for history and being a genuine supportive person.

To Norton for making dreams come true for me and many other people. To my editors Stephanie Derhak and John Toren—I appreciate your talent. John did a great job in helping me to shape the book and made it look good. A tough collaborative effort, but well worth it.

To my family for their support and love, especially my daughter-in-law Melanie Kieley for her excellent photography, constant support and creative spirit. You are a joy to have around and your photographs made the book come alive. To Joe, DJ, Anthony, & Sammy, I love you all. To Doug for the last minute editing, quick photos, putting up with crummy meals and most of all for sharing my journey from the beginning to the end celebration. You are the Best!

TABLE OF CONTENTS

Introduction

2 School and Neighborhood

My School Memories / Child of the 50s / Jump Rope Rhymes / My Love for Paper Dolls /
The Lennon Sisters / My Bride Doll / Sharing a Bike / My Best Friend and First Crush /
Penny Candy in a Brown Paper Sack / Old Fashioned Candy / Cowboy Shows, Monster Movies
and Playing Ball in the Street / F & M School Savings Program

18 The Rise of TV: Entertainment for the Whole Family

Family sitcoms / TV Westerns / Fury / The Rifleman / American Bandstand / Dobie Gillis /
My Little Margie / The Real McCoys / Lassie

28 What We Wore

Teenage Fashions in the 1950s / Junior High / American Bandstand Sets the Standards / Fashion in the 1960's /
Sewing and Home Ec. / Fashion Sewing in the 1960s / Amluxen's and Learning to Sew / My Sewing Machine /
Newspaper Patterns / Prom was a Special Night / Charm Bracelets / Crinolines / Hot Pants /
Go-Go Boots / Mohair Sweaters / The Shirtwaisted Woman / Padded Bras / Nylons / Girdles

50 Hair

Hair Dye / How to Create a French Roll / Beehive / The Breck Girl / The First Home Permanents

58 What Our Parents Wore: Hats, Aprons, and Housedresses

Aprons / Full Aprons / Hostess Aprons / Kitsch and Novelty Aprons / Gingham Aprons / Crocheted Apron /
Housedresses / Hats / Hankies

68 Drive-Ins: The Place to Be on a Saturday Night

Twin City Drive-In Theatres / Twin City Drive-in Movie Locations / Pretending to be the Singing Popcorn Box /
A Tank of My Own / Porky's Drive In / The First Frosty Mug / Bridgeman's

82 **Put on Your Gloves Let's Go Downtown**

Going Downtown with My Sister / History of Downtown Stores / Young Quinlan / The Fountain Tea Room /Donaldson's Glass Block / Daytons / Eighth Floor Auditorium / Santa Bear /Holly Bell / Teen Board / Penney's / Powers / Ending of Downtown Shopping Era / Chandler Shoes / Amluxen's / The Nankin Restaurant / Working at the Nankin / The Forum Cafeteria

108 **Dime Store Dreams**

Kresge's /Grant's / Woolworth's / Photo Machines / Closing of the Dime Stores: The End of an Era

118 **Music**

My Love for Music / Patrol Picnic / School Dances / The Day John F Kennedy was Shot / The Beatles on the Ed Sullivan Show / Viet Nam 1969 / Hit Parade 1950s: From Pop to Rock / Dances / Local Bands of the Sixties / Transistor Radios / Popular Radio Stations

134 **Freebies and Fads**

Saving for my Hope Chest / S & H Green Stamps / Gold Bond Stamps / Free Glassware and Towels / Betty Crocker Coupons / Depression Glass / How Cracker Jack Began / Northern Girls / Day of the Week Panties / Princess Phone / Evening in Paris Perfume / Pop-It Beads / Pajama Parties / Lane Cedar Chests / A Gift from the Orient / Slam books / Catalogs / Cereal Box Prizes

150 **Attics, Pantries and Traditions**

Melmac Dishes / The Pantry / The Attic / The Basement / Traditions A Chore for Every Day / Christmas When I was Growing Up / A Fifties Christmas / Remember Aluminum Christmas Trees? / Memories of Christmases Past

160 **Classic Cars and Drag Racing**

Hot Rod Fever / Muscle Cars of the 1960s / Cruisin' and Racin' in the Fifties / Car Clubs / Car Parts and Gear

172 **A Photographic Stroll Down Memory Lane**

182 **Photo Credits, Index, About the Author**

Green Stamps
to Hot Pants

INTRODUCTION

I have fond memories of my childhood years. But it also makes me a little sad when I think back because times have changed so much and so quickly. Although I am not that old it seems like I grew up a hundred years ago. It's been said that people waste time dreaming about yesterday; but there is a piece of me that remains back there.

I remember the day we moved into our house in Northeast Minneapolis and how it seemed so strange to me, so unknown; an old house that smelled of wooden floors and linoleum. There were freshly planted little trees and railroad tracks in the field across the street. We were near the Mississippi River, with a park that had swings, a slide, monkey-bars and a wading pool. My brother and I hid in the coal bin and built forts across the street. My mother cooked great meals of fried chicken or Sunday roast beef with mashed potatoes and white cream gravy, peas and carrots and her special home made bread that she baked fresh each week. My brother and I sat cross-legged and wide-eyed on the living room floor watching the cowboy shows on Saturday mornings.

The neighborhood was alive with a pulse all its own. We got to know the kids on our block; the Anderson, Rosti and Dalecki girls with their swing set in the backyard. I envied them. Mothers screamed out their front door for their kids to come in for supper. We sat down together to eat and said Grace. After supper we ran and played Red Light, Green Light, Statue, King of the Mountain, catch and bounce the ball, sang songs and played lots of make believe. We'd leave our windows and doors wide open during summer nights so we'd get the cool breezes going through. No one had air-conditioning in those days.

We sometimes lay down on the grass to look at the stars. We'd see who could find the big and little dippers, and of course we'd wish on a star. The seasons came and went. In the summer we played marbles, jump rope, and practiced tricks with our yo-yos. In the winter we made snow angels and skated at the park. I remember catching raindrops in my mouth and eating snow and icicles. We had time to dream and to be together.

September brought school and a new excitement. The thrill of brand-new clothes and school supplies; how great was that! We piled up leaves and dove into them and enjoyed the paper sales and ice cream socials. We went through good times and bad. Went through friendships new and old, first loves, first heartbreaks, sock hops and doo-wop music. We danced our hearts out, traded clothes and our 45s. I'll always remember that time. Like many other baby boomers I have a deep sentimental yearning to reclaim the memory of days long past. We were the "Baby Boom Generation" born after the soldiers had come home from World War II, 1946 to 1962. No matter how ridiculous or dowdy we looked back then, it was the way we were. As teenagers we used words like "far out" and "cool" and "groovy," and some of us became rebels, protesting the Viet Nam War, cultivating Flower Power, and adopting the Hippie lifestyle. The music was deep, powerful and also a little crazy.

But it was also a time of innocence; this is a memoir of the world as I remember it in the 1950s and 60s.

Chapter 1 : **School and Neighborhood**

My School Memories

My life in the city began abruptly. On the day my dad died we were whisked off the farm right in the middle of the school day and taken to the big city of Minneapolis, more than a hundred miles away. The fast pace of city life was much like a foreign country to a six-year-old girl who was used to a one room school and an outdoor bathroom.

I don't know quite how I balanced it all. I loved my father more than anything in the world. Suddenly he was gone, and we were forced to move away from the only place I knew. Our back yard was next to the Mud River, which wound its way from the lake down under the bridge and then meandered off through fields and trees for as far as the eye could see. But my new home in the city was smack dab in the middle of a residential area with an alley and houses on each side of us. The school was two blocks away, and it was so scary when I first went there. It had ten classrooms on two floors and seemed huge to me. It was going up and down the stairs that mixed me up. I kept getting lost.

We didn't really have new clothes to wear. My mother got boxes of clothes from somewhere. We just picked out the best ones and tried to make the best of it. We were thrilled to have them because we didn't know any other way. Luckily when my older sisters got jobs in downtown Minneapolis years later, they would buy clothes for us younger ones.

On the first day of school, my mother introduced me to my first grade teacher, Mrs. Mary Lennon. Strangely enough, she had also been my mother's first grade teacher. My mother was born in 1904, so needless to say that was a long time ago. We didn't have kindergarten in the one room school I went to on the farm. I was in first grade and I was a little jealous at times because the kindergarteners had a real cool room that we were allowed to visit on occasion. They had a sandbox and a swing set with a jungle gym right in the middle of the classroom. But the kindergarten teacher was old Mrs. Ester Lennon and she was the crabby one—not at all like her sister Mary, who was very sweet. I was always glad I got Mary and that my mother had her too.

Our Christmases were very meager when I lived on the farm. There were not a lot of goodies baked since we

had very little food for a family of seven. We were each given a pair of colorful anklets by our parents, of which one sock was filled with peanuts and the other a piece of fruit. One year my family received a Croquet set and a Monopoly game that we played almost every day because we had no other toys.

This may explain why the classroom Christmas parties in the city were especially magical for me. One year every student in my class was given an individually wrapped gift. Can you imagine the surprise in my little girl eyes when I opened the glittered star package with the shiny bow. It was my very own ceramic Christmas Angel, and I cherish it to this day. She had blonde hair and blue eyes just the way I imagined an angel to be. My brother got a choir boy that was dressed in the red skirt of an altar boy. (I'm not sure he was as thrilled as I was.) The culmination of the party was when I got sick from

eating too many Christmas cookies and my teacher had to drive me home. I was going to love city life!

The teachers in this neighborhood school were especially nice and I remember their kindness still even though it was almost fifty years ago. They had a way of including me in things even though I was extremely shy. I was a dreamer and liked to draw pictures. They praised me for my artwork and assigned me special projects making posters and murals. I wonder sometimes if the drawings were really that good or if these teachers simply had a compassionate heart and a love for children.

In the late summer time we would spend hours raking leaves and then jump into the huge piles we'd amassed from the school yard trees.

Child of the 50s

I was a child of the 50s. I had just turned seven when we moved from the farm in 1956. I grew up in a typical city neighborhood. The streets were pretty quiet except when the freight trains came by, at least every hour. The houses were built close together. You could look right into the neighbor's windows from our house, but we never did. The neighbors were friendly and always said Hi as I walked down the alley. Our house was the oldest on the block. To get to the basement there was a trapdoor on the back porch—a very scary trap door.

We had wide sidewalks and elm trees lining the boulevard. Almost everyone had a garden in the back yard and fruit trees. People sat on their front porches and watched what was going on in the world of our neighborhood.

Our family took Sunday drives just for something

to do. We had a group of five girls that would play together. Our routine was to play House or School, paper dolls or cards, taking turns at each person's house. We played many card games like Crazy Eights or Casino but War was the favorite. We'd have our little tournaments using two decks. We'd call some of the cards by special names. The ace of spades was "Gary." Everyone loved to get Gary because he was the cutest boy in the neighborhood. We played it out putting the cards down fast and then pouncing when there was a war. As the players were eliminated they became onlookers and cheered us on. We took this seriously and the champ was given a great deal of honor and admiration. They got to choose the game we would play for the next time or they got to be the hero in our pretend games.

At night sometimes we'd play Red Light: Green Light, Statue, or Starlight, Moonlight, a game of tag. We liked the running games the most. Sometimes we would ask the boys from the neighborhood to play with us. Cowboys and Indians or Army were the boy's favorite games and there was never a hint of avoiding violence for them. They had their play guns and their plastic army men. They would beg us girls to play those games and sometimes we would oblige. We played Marbles for hours. And then there was Jax, Hopscotch, Jump Rope and Four Square. A game of throwing a ball in the air and catching it was called Plainseys, Clapseys. Also we played One, Two, Three a Larry and some times Annie,

Annie Over. But it made our parents nervous to have us throwing a ball over their roof, so that never lasted long. Chinese jump rope was a craze for several years. It involved different ways of using your feet to jump with a rope made of several rubber bands tied together. These ropes were very colorful. I still remember some of the rhymes we chanted as we jumped.

Jump Rope

Although girls sometimes jumped individually, they more often jumped in groups, with several girls sharing one long rope. When boys jumped, they usually joined a group of girls. Two girls were the "enders," who turned the rope; the other girls were the jumpers. There was some competition, for every girl wanted to be the best jumper. But also cooperation; because the enders had to turn evenly and rhythmically so the jumpers could do their best. Then, when the enders' turn to jump came, their friends would turn as well for them.

As the girls jumped they made an art as well as a sport of the game; they reinvented the jump-rope rhyme. Rhymes helped the enders keep the rhythm and they also lent poetry and humor to the game. The games of Straight Jumping and How Many proposed a challenge to see how many times you could jump without missing. In the game of Red Hot Peppers, the enders would twirl the rope very fast whenever the word pepper came up, in an effort to make the jumper miss. Actions and commands meant you had to do some things like turn around, touch the ground or do the splits. Yes, No or Maybe included rhymes that asked a question such as

Jump Rope Rhymes

Bluebells, cockle shells, eevy, ivy, OVER
One, two, three, four, five, six, seven
All good children go to heaven
I love coffee, I love tea
Cinderella dressed in yellow
Down in the valley where the green grass grows
Mabel, Mabel, set the table
Johnny over the ocean
I told Mama and Mama told Papa
I'm a little Dutch girl
Spanish dancer, do the splits
Teddy bear, teddy bear turn around
Fudge, fudge, tell the judge
Blondie and Dagwood went to town
Strawberry shortcake, blueberry pie
Not last night but the night before
Sheep in the meadow, cows in the corn

"What does your doll eat for breakfast?" followed by a list of answers—colors, houses, or numbers. The word you missed on answered the question. Name Your Sweetheart predicted the name of your future sweetheart by giving the letters of his name. In and Out let the jumper call in a friend by name. All in Together meant all the girls could jump in at once.

My Love for Paper Dolls and the Lennon Sisters

I loved paper dolls. You could get them in any store and they were reasonably priced. My favorites were June Allyson and Janet Lennon from the Lawrence Welk Show. The Lawrence Welk Show was a variety show with singing, dancing and big band music that aired every Saturday night. I don't know that I liked the show so much but I loved the Lennon Sisters. In frilly feminine dresses they sang their hearts out in beautiful harmony. You could tell Lawrence Welk had a fondness for Janet, the youngest, and he often gave her special interviews. We watched her grow up on TV. Later books were written about Janet and her adventures and her life on the show.

Paper Dolls

Paper dolls have existed as long as there has been paper and creative people to apply images to it. A paper doll is a two-dimensional figure drawn or printed on paper for which accompanying clothing has also been provided. It's a flat paper object, but provides a great deal of pleasure! Popular figures from opera, stage, screen and

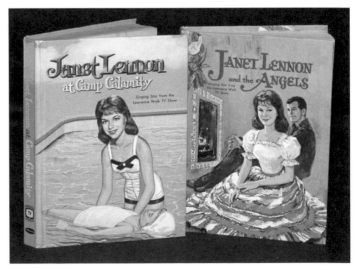

even television have appeared as paper dolls. Royalty and political figures also appear as paper dolls. Paper dolls have always been one of the cheapest, but most fascinating toys of childhood.

In the 1820s, boxed paper doll sets were popularly produced in Europe and exported to America. The 1900s saw an explosion of paper dolls in many lady's and children's magazines. The fashion magazine the Delineator by Butterick Patterns featured a charming series of three-dimensional wraparound dolls. Paper dolls that were accompanied by toys, theaters and stories inspired patriotism during World War I.

Who doesn't know Betsy McCall, perhaps the best known magazine paper doll in America? She came along after a long tradition of paper dolls in McCall's from 1904 to 1926 featuring the Jack and Jill Twins, Teeny Town, villages, dolls and furniture, the Nipper series, and clever cut-and-fold McCall Family series.

Sweet-faced Betsy McCall by Kay Morrissey debuted in 1951. Betsy McCall modeled fashions that could be made with McCall's patterns while she enjoyed travels and activities. Betsy has come and gone from the 1960s with various changes in style, from the 1970s "mod" look to modern Betsy in the late 1990s.

When paper dolls surged in popularity, manufacturers of all kinds of household goods took advantage of them to promote their wares. A few of the products advertised with paper dolls were Lyon's coffee, Pillsbury flour, Baker's chocolate, Singer sewing machines, Clark's threads, McLaughlin coffee and Hood's Sarsaparilla. Later, companies put paper dolls into their magazine advertisements to sell goods such as nail polish, underwear, Spring maid fabrics, Quadriga Cloth, Ford Cars, Fels Naphtha and Swan soaps, Carter's clothing for children, and more.

The 1930s through the 1950s have perhaps claimed the title "Golden Age of Paper Dolls," as their popularity in those years has never been equaled. During the Great Depression everyone could afford paper toys. Despite the product shortages of World War II, paper dolls were still manufactured, though on lesser-quality papers. Parents of the 1950s re-

vered the image of little girls lovingly playing with paper dolls, just as their mothers and grandmothers had done before them.

Celebrities and movie stars were very popular with all the major publishers. It was much simpler to portray stars in the 1930s, 1940s and 1950s when rights were generally not secured. Studios often "owned" movie stars and their images, and the stars themselves never saw any income from their sale as paper dolls. With images of beloved stars and sports heroes protected today, a publisher must pay for the rights to reproduce our favorite stars as paper dolls.

My Bride Doll

For my ninth birthday my sister bought two identical bride dolls from our neighborhood grocery and variety store; one for her and one for me. They were each displayed in a box covered with cellophane and wore a white veil and lace-trimmed wedding dress. Mine even had a bouquet tied to her small hand. I remember her netted stockings and white plastic shoes with straps, and that her eyes opened and closed.

I loved my doll so much that I played with her constantly. The bride's dress, although beautiful, didn't stay on for long. She was always dressed in the latest of fashions with clothes that I sewed for her myself, though my methods were primitive. Sitting up in the attic, I used stickpins and safety pins for fastening the remnants of old clothes to her body. She became a masterpiece dressed in leftovers from many different eras.

She and I spent hours of make believe together. She could travel to places I would never see. She had curly blonde hair that mimicked the style of the 1950s, when ladies wore their hair in a bubble cut tightly curled from home permanents. But I had soon rubbed most of her hair off by washing and combing it repeatedly. So I began fashioning hair ornaments to cover up her bald spot. I used a tassel belt from my older sister's cast-off winter coat. Two furry tassels hung at the end of a turquoise wool belt. I made bows and braids and anything else I could think of to pin on top. I sat playing with my doll for hours and would get lost in her pretend world. My mother used to say it was because I loved my doll so much that her hair fell out.

One time I thought she needed rubber pants so I sneaked into the bathroom and cut off the bottom of the green plastic window curtains, which had pink flamingos painted on them. I was sure no one would notice a piece was gone since the bottom was cut in a straight line-- well almost! I didn't see why my mother was so upset about it. This was the only real doll I ever had and she needed clothes. I'm not sure what happened to her; probably she just got thrown away.

My sister still has her bride doll. She is in perfect condition in the cellophane see- through box. She did have to replace the bride's dress because the fabric had deteriorated from age. Even things that aren't over-loved fall apart. She kept her doll on a shelf only for looks and never played with her. Sometimes I wish I had left mine in the box, but then I would never have learned to love her.

Though my sister's doll was identical to mine I don't feel the same when I see her. Perhaps she is too perfect. I wish I still had my doll; I miss her.

My favorite teddy bear drowned in my sister's flooded basement and she had to throw him away. Sometimes I feel a terrible sadness over the loss of my two favorite childhood playthings; as though somehow I might recapture my childhood if only I could touch my teddy bear and my bride doll one more time.

Sharing a Bike

It was during the summer of 1960 that I learned to ride a bike, thanks to Laurie and Joannie, two friends that lived on California Street. They went to the Catholic school and I went to the public, but on weekends they wore regular clothes and there were no differences between us.

The two of them shared a bike that was a real sleek machine. It was made of lime green heavy-gauge steel with an oversized basket in front and a special bucking bumper in the back that was long and sturdy. Even though these girls were two and three years younger than I was they were extremely patient and willing to share their bike with me. The two of them would take turns running along the side of the bike, giving me a shove so that I could peddle by myself down the boulevard. Months went by before I got the hang of it. I was scared

hopping on this bike that was so much bigger than I was and in motion besides. The fear of going so fast was extreme but I was excited too.

The elm trees near the street made the going even worse, and the ever-present sidewalk seemed to rise up from beneath me and meet my falls. That year I had so many bruises on my knees and legs that the wounds barely healed before I skinned them again. Scabs became a way of life. Sometimes a kid's legs are held together by scabs.

It seemed to take forever for me to learn how to ride, but my playmates did not give up on me. We'd just get started and much too soon their mother would call them to come in. I still remember Mrs. Dalecki calling out the door for them. "Laurie Ann…..Joannie Marie….." She would sing out, and their names would echo down the street or the alley. Later, when their little brother came along, the name Albin was tacked onto the "name" jingle. But this time she sang in a more masculine tone.

Conquering the two-wheeler and learning to steer it meant freedom and independence. Laurie and Joannie were always supportive. Never once did they say, "You're getting pretty old to be learning how to ride a bike." It took a lot of determination. I was shy about a lot of things but once I learned to ride that bike I became a bolder person.

But then another problem arose. Three people sharing a bike was not an ideal situation. The fact that they were younger and couldn't come out to play as often as I could, and had to go in earlier, also made it more difficult.

For my birthday that year, I received a real surprise. My mother bought me my own blue bicycle. My life took on another new dimension. My bike was old long before it had reached my hands by merit of a flea market; but I loved this bike and treated it as if it were new. For years it was my ticket to freedom. I spent many days riding around the block and to the park.

My Best Friend and First Crush

I met my first real best friend in sixth grade. Pat and I were inseparable. We spent every day together. She would call and say, "Meet you half way," and I would say, "Okay." Then I would saunter down the alley behind our house heading towards 28th and California Street where she lived. Sometimes there would be a mix up and she would come down California while I made my way down the alley and we would end up missing each other all together. Then one of us would have to stay put and wait for the other to come looking. We always laughed because we had forgotten to say which way we were coming.

We dressed almost exactly alike most of the time in oversized men's shirts, knee knockers and bobby sox. But we had one outfit that we especially picked out together—black culottes and a turquoise double-breasted flowered jacket. We thought we were the ultimate of cool. The only difference between us was that she filled her jacket out on top more than I did.

Our favorite spot to go was the park. We sat on the swings for hours and sang songs. We knew all the words to "Travellin' Man" by Ricky Nelson. And we even harmonized the lyrics a little. Sometimes I would do tricks on the parallel bars and she would stand nearby and watch me. I was a little more athletic than her. I'd hang on those bars for the longest time. But we had to keep on our guard in case a group of boys from the neighborhood

decided they wanted to have a little fun. They'd sneak up behind us and throw us into the pool. For some reason they always wanted to throw Pat in the pool. I guess it was because they wanted to see what she looked like when her shirt got wet.

Pat and I remained best friends throughout the years. We even fell in love with the same guy. She kept talking about Jeff so much; how he pushed his blonde hair out of his eyes, how cute he talked, the way he held a basketball and how he looked in his red jacket. I heard so much about him, I started to fall in love with him myself.

It was the day of the school Ice Cream Social, one of the biggest events of the year, other than Field Day. It was a fund raiser for the school. Everyone came out to enjoy ice cream during the heat of the summer.

All day I thought I would burst with this wonderful thing inside me. I knew I had to tell someone. At the end of the night, Pat and I stood near the playground fence discussing the excitement of the day. I was so sure that I would break Pat's heart if I told her I was in love with the same boy. I figured she would never speak to me again. But it seemed like such a perfect night that I found my courage. It cooled down just enough to make the air smell fresh. Suddenly I found myself spilling out everything.

She didn't get upset, but in fact was excited. She insisted this way we could work on him together. But, what was supposed to be a dual effort for the affections of Jeff inevitably became a competition. Jeff was in the seventh grade, so in one way Pat had the advantage, as she could wear make up and was much more endowed, so she looked older than I did. But I had something she couldn't compete with. I had my own basketball, a sure pathway to Jeff's heart. And even better than that, I knew how to use it. I started calling him up and asking him if he wanted to shoot baskets. He usually said "Sure," so we'd meet over at the school that was a few blocks away. We always played HORSE or PIG, a game where you took the letter of an animal every time you missed a basket. The first one to get all the letters was the loser. My brother taught me how to sink a basket and with more practice I was getting pretty good at it. My record was at least two out of three. Jeff and I didn't talk much; we just shot baskets for a half-hour or so, and then went home.

I started playing baseball after supper at the school playground with some of my brother's friends, including Jeff and his brother. I was sure that Jeff was impressed because I was always the first girl to be picked. Of course, the other girls didn't really try very hard and were afraid of falling or getting dirty. They didn't seem to know much about the game either. Pat didn't even care to learn.

One evening we were playing dodge ball in the alley behind Jeff's house. Suddenly the idea got around that I wanted to kiss Jeff and so did Pat. I was pretty scared, but I thought this would be a wonderful opportunity. I would never do it otherwise. It was getting late and we were finishing up the game, I had been hit by the ball and was out. So I ran up, kissed him on the cheek and said goodbye. I suppose you could say I had a head rush but mostly because I had to do it so quickly.

I really don't remember ever falling out of love with Jeff. I guess when I went to junior high the next year, I found out how he acted on the bus. He smoked and used a lot of filthy words and hung out with skuzzy people. I

guess I realized that his pretty face and nice body shape were really the only things he had. Inside he was a real scuz-bucket. By the way, his real name wasn't even Jeff, it was Kenley. He got the name Jeff because he had gotten a pair of hand-me-down pajamas with the name Jeff stamped on them.

PENNY CANDY IN A BROWN PAPER SACK

Linda Petroske

Eddy's Grocery Store on 33rd and Stinson Boulevard was the best place to get penny candy. The glass candy jars in the front window would entice me in. Eddy would hand you a small paper bag that you could choose whatever candies you wanted. After filling it, we'd tell Eddy how many pieces were in the bag and pay him accordingly. If he caught you lying about how much you took, you would have to earn his respect back. The next time you went in to visit, you would have to promise him you would never do it again. "Do you have too much in there? I'm going to have to take it if I can't trust you," he'd say in front of all the waiting customers.

More of Linda's Memories

Linda Petroske

"We had a trap door that went to a cellar with a dirt floor. That's where we kept potatoes and onions for winter. They were stored in bags or bins. It was really cold down there. Grandma said to never clean the dirt off the vegetables or they would never grow again. There was canning stuff down there too.

My brother made up a game where he would take a U-shaped magnet and pick up items from my metal tea set on a string that he dangled over the banister of an open stairway. He fished for things that way for hours. My brother also used to swear as he was putting on his cowboy boots. Grandma often carried a bar of soap in her apron pocket. He would ask her, "Do you have your bar of soap with you, Grandma?" He knew he couldn't swear if she did.

The Gold Bond Redemption Center was the greatest store on Highway 55 and County Road 9. The building had a huge arch on it. It's still there but now it's called the Carlson Company. Mom had a special box in the kitchen with a handle on it that she used to store stamps."

Remember These?

Old Fashioned Candy

Candy buttons, Atomic Fireballs, Bit-O-Honey, Black Crows, Boston Baked Beans, Boyers Mallo Cups, candy cigarettes, candy lipstick (taffy style and Sweetart style), candy necklace, Chick-O-Stix, cherry mash, Charms Assorted Squares, Chuckles Jelly Candy, Dots, Goobers, Good N Plenty, jawbreakers, Jujubes, junior mints, Kits taffy, Lemonheads, licorice pipes, licorice wheel, licorice babies, Lik-M-Aid, Milk Duds, Mary Janes, Necco Wafers, Nik-L-Nip Wax Bottles, Pixy Stix, Pop rocks, Raisinettes, Red Hots, Root beer barrels, Sen-Sen, Slo-Pokes, Smarties, Snaps, Scooter Pies, Sno-caps, Tootsie Roll Pop, Tootsie Roll Fudge, Sugar Babies, Sweetarts, wax lips, wax mustaches and Whoppers.

Candy Bars

Seven Up Bar (it had seven different sections, with seven different candies), Sky Bar, 5th Avenue, Bing, Heath Bar,

Pay Day, Hundred Thousand Dollar Bar/100 Grand, Clark Bar, Baby Ruth, Butterfinger, Milkshake Bar, Snickers Bars, Three Musketeers, Neapolitan Coconut Bars, Chunky, Look Bar, Marathon Bar (8" of braided chocolate and caramel), Mounds, Almond Joy, O Henry, Zagnut, Zero!

Gum

Clark Teabury Gum, Fruit Striped, Chiclets, Black Jack, Clove, Beamans, Cadbury, Clove, Wrigley's Spearment, Double Mint, Juicy Fruit, and Bazooka bubble gum

Old Fashioned Pop

Frostie Root Beer, Nesbitt's of California, Coca-Cola, R C Cola, Pepsi, Nehi [in various flavors], 7-up, Dr.Pepper, Bubble-Up, Shasta, Tab, Fresca, Hires Root Beer, A&W Root Beer, Mug Root Beer, Canada Dry Ginger Ale, Brownie Root Beer, Squirt, Nehi soda, Orange Crush, Grape Crush, and Mason's Root Beer.

Cowboy Shows, Monster Movies and Playing Ball in the Street

Doug Kieley

LIKE MANY OTHER KIDS growing up in the 50s, I was mesmerized by the TV set for hours on Saturday mornings. Cowboy shows were super popular and we wanted to be just like the heroes of the shows. Some of my favorites were the Lone Ranger, Bat Masterson, Paladin, Rifleman, the Rebel, Yancy Derringer, Roy Rogers and Sky King. I also liked Gunsmoke. I wore my cowboy hat and boots while I was watching. I'd be all duded up in a fringe jacket with two six guns in a double holster made of real leather with bullet loops for the silver bullets. I had a rifle that was just like the Rifleman's and I would stand in front of the TV and flip it around, twirl it, and shoot caps. I also had a snub nose 38 with shoulder holster that would shoot shells. We were told it could put someone's eye out. Before long they had taken it off the market. *(continued next page)*

I also had a derringer that was built in to my belt buckle, just like Bat Masterson. Or I could wear it on a spring-loaded device that would flip it into my hand at a moment's notice. When I stuck my tummy out, the derringer would pop forward out of the buckle and plastic bullets would go flying. The weapon was spring-loaded with Mattel Shoot 'um Shells and Greenie Stick 'um Caps.

At the beginning of each episode of *Gunsmoke*, Matt Dillon killed someone. I would stand there with two six guns, ready to draw and shoot. I could always beat Matt. I'd shoot the bad guy, then I'd shoot Matt too.

My friends and I played Cowboys and Indians all the time. We made our own bow and arrows. Dale Evans gear for girls was popular and Roy Rogers and Davy Crocket paraphernalia was cool for boys. Almost every kid had Hop Along Cassidy guns and a Davy Crocket hat.

Saturday movies were big pastimes for kids too. My friends and I would walk down to the Broadway, Paradise, or Empress theater where you could see a double feature or triple feature for only twenty cents. First they would show the newsreel, then the cartoon, and finally the feature movie. We mostly liked the monster/horror movies like the Blob, Teenage Werewolf, House on Haunted Hill, Thirteen Ghosts, and Creature from the Black Lagoon. Monster on Campus was the favorite because we would laugh at the phoniness of the crooked hand wearing a rubber glove. It would be an all-afternoon event. A box of popcorn and a box of candy would last quite a while. The Paradise was a really old theater with castles built into the walls and lights in the windows and balconies. Later they remodeled it and took all that neat stuff out.

Kids would get pretty rowdy and sometimes hit the usher in the head with a jawbreaker. Every once in a while they'd stop the movie right in the middle and the usher would get on the mike and yell, "Keep quiet, settle down!" The kids would boo, hiss, and scream. They even threw gum balls at the screen. Then the usher would say, "I've got all day if you don't want to be quiet." Eventually the crowd would quiet down and the movie would start up again.

We played a lot of board games and Hide and Go Seek. Other popular toys were Erector sets, classic car model kits, Lincoln logs, Tinker toys, electric trains, wind up toys, and comic books. And we all rode our bikes.

I feel sad that the kids of today can't enjoy unplanned fun the way we did.

There were very few organized sports in those days. We could almost always get together a group of guys from the neighborhood to play ball. A vacant lot, in the street, the park, front yards, wherever we could find a spot. There were no umpires, no coaches, and no parents telling us what to do. You just had to get along on your own and it taught you something. It was more fun that way. Parents weren't necessary. Sure there were a few fights and bloody noses once in awhile, but you learned how to work things out. We knew how to create our own fun. We built forts on the garage roof, climbed trees, and ran free all day long. We always had some kind of adventure going.

Pennies Saved:
F & M School Savings Program

The Farmers and Mechanics Mutual Savings Bank was started in 1874. One of the bank's most enduring legacies was the School Savings Program, through which, for nearly 75 years, school children in Minneapolis learned about thrift and the benefits of saving their hard earned pennies, nickels, and dimes.

Long before the bank got involved, Grace Livingston started a program called the Provident Savings System, taking house-to-house collections from families. She believed that the only way families could save money was to encourage thrift among the children. She was right.

If you grew up in Minneapolis, you probably remember when it was bank day at school and you had to bum a nickel or dime from the kid next to you to deposit in your savings account. One hundred percent participation was important for the school and sometimes your room even won a prize.

Collections for the children's savings accounts were taken at several central libraries, nine missions, three settlement houses, and ten schools. F & M, as it was popularly known, took over management of the program in 1908. Many classrooms had a student monitor who helped the teacher collect money on "bank day." There was no minimum for saving. At least a nickel every time was preferred, but if the kids put in pennies the transaction had to be recorded.

During the Depression and war years, saving money and being thrifty became a national pastime, and the school savings program continued to prosper after the

war. In 1958, there were 159 metropolitan schools participating, and more than 80 percent of the students and teachers had accounts. The bank had long used a dog in its advertising to symbolize the safety of its deposits, and when the school savings program was at its peak, the dog was joined by a young girl, symbolizing the school savings program.

The school bank located in Minneapolis was on the second floor, with a mural of children around the walls and a recessed floor behind the tellers' stations to make the tellers appear shorter for the children. There were regular tours of the bank. The students could look in the vaults, see a movie, ogle big bills and eat ice cream. Sometimes the kids sent letters and gave their opinion of the bank. One of them said, "I'll never wash my hands after touching that thousand-dollar bill."

Parents sometimes tried to talk the tellers into letting them take money out without the child's signature. Their hard-luck stories were sometimes compelling, but it was strictly against the bank's rules.

During the late 1960s participation began to decline and balances dropped. It seemed the entire nation had lost interest in saving money. In 1973 the school savings program was discontinued and its accounts were converted into passbook savings accounts. Yet though the program no longer exists, the values that it promoted have endured and the memories it inspired live on.

Chapter 2

THE RISE OF TV:
ENTERTAINMENT FOR THE WHOLE FAMILY

Although television shows were produced on an experimental basis in the 1940s, few families had TVs in those days, and it was not until the 1950s that television became a source of widespread entertainment for both kids and adults. During the 1950s Americans put the traumas of a world war behind them and "normal" family life was a much-coveted ideal. In many households the TV set became the center of the living area. In the evenings the whole family would pile on the davenport or curl up on the floor in front of it. As the technology improved, the TV set gradually grew in size, up to a glorious 21 inches! During this time console TVs were made to look like streamlined wooden furniture. Continental-crafted models with knobs and speakers were a sign of prestige and people started buying them. The "home entertainment center," with radio, phonograph and television all in one unit, was the ultimate. Magnavox, Admiral, Zenith, GE, Curtis Mathis, Motorola and Philco were major brands.

As more households purchased TV sets, more programs were produced— westerns, variety shows, Saturday morning cartoons, and the Saturday series. Advertisers were quick to recognize the new medium's potential, and soon every kid wanted to buy Davy Crockett hats, Roy Roger's gun sets, and Ovaltine. It was a great method of selling. The host of a show would announce a commercial then walk over and sell the product himself.

Saturday and Sunday nights were TV family nights. On Saturday, the *Red Skelton Show* was popular. Sunday evenings were devoted to the *Ed Sullivan Show*, followed by *Walt Disney's Wonderful World of Color*. When Tinkerbell came to introduce the show and they played the song, "When you wish upon a star," your heart would melt. There was such a magic and wonder in this program. Other popular weekend shows during the early years of TV were *Loretta Young, Lawrence Welk, Mitch Miller, I've Got a Secret, 77 Sunset Strip, To Tell the Truth, My Favorite Martian, Laugh In, the Smothers Brothers* and *The Real McCoys*.

Kids' Shows

Television shows for kids appeared almost as soon as TV went on the air. *The Howdy Doody Show* started in 1947, featuring Clarabelle the Clown. Other kiddy favorites included *Ding Dong School, Romper Room, The Pinky Lee Show*, and *Kukla, Fran, and Ollie*. In 1955, Bob Keeshan, who had played Clarabelle the Clown, started his own show called *Captain Kangaroo*. Keeshan won awards for his show because he put the needs of the children ahead of the demands of the sponsors.

Saturday morning cartoons such as CBS's *Mighty Mouse Playhouse* were first aired in 1955. That year, ABC premiered the hour-long *Mickey Mouse Club*. This program introduced Walt Disney to American children. The show only ran until 1959, but was by far the most popular children's show. Fan mail poured in from across the country at a rate of seventy-five hundred letters a month. Kids across the nation tuned in to see their favorite Mouseketeers perform skits and sing songs.

Other Saturday Morning shows were *Rifleman, Fury, Wagon Train, My Friend Flicka, Lassie, Howdy Doody, Andy Divine, Sky King*, and *Roy Rogers*. The after-school shows were *Mickey Mouse Club, Axel* and cartoons which included Mighty Mouse, Tom and Jerry, Road Runner and Donald Duck.

Family sitcoms

Some of the most popular family sitcoms were the *Danny Thomas Show, My Three Sons, Father Knows Best, Donna Reed Show, Leave it to Beaver*, the *Patty Duke Show, Petty Coat Junction, Family Affair, December Bride*, and *Dobie Gillis*. These shows were initially scheduled for weekday evenings, though some were later syndicated in the after-school line up.

TV Westerns

TV Westerns reigned supreme in the Fifties and early Sixties. There were about 120 of them depending on what you considered a Western. Like the post-war world in which they flourished, you could always tell the good guys from the bad. And none of the guns were fully automatic.

The earliest TV Westerns were mostly kiddy fare, typified by Roy Rogers. In the mid-Fifties *Gunsmoke* began its 20-year run. It was the first successful "adult" Western. As fast as you could say, "they went thataway, pardner" the airwaves were filled with Westerns. A long running favorite, *Wagon Train*, debuted in 1957 along with *Maverick* and *Have Gun Will Travel*.

Studios quickly realized that the Western didn't just appeal to men, and accordingly cast hunky leads, who often appeared shirtless to please the women. No longer did the hero kiss his horse and ride off into the sunset. Now he got to kiss the girl instead!

Other well known Westerns were *Adventures of Jim Bowie, Annie Oakley, Cisco Kid, Cheyenne, Davy Crocket*,

THE RISE OF TV

Death Valley Days, Wyatt Earp, Gene Autry, Gunsmoke, Hopalong Cassidy, Lawman, Rawhide, Rebel, Rin Tin Tin, Johnny Ringo, Rough Riders, Roy Rogers and Dale Evans, Sheriff of Cochise, Sky King, Wanted Dead or Alive, and *Wild Bill Hickok.*

By the Sixties, the Westerns, led by ratings winner *Bonanza,* began broadcasting in color. *The Virginian, High Chaparral,* and *Big Valley* were typical. But as the decade progressed the simple verities provided by the Wild West no longer struck a chord, and as the decade drew to a close, the TV Western had all but disappeared.

The Rifleman

9/30/1958-7/13/1963 ABC
Black and White-30 minutes-169 episodes

Cast
   Chuck Connors as Lucas McCain
   Johnny Crawford as Mark McCain
   Paul Fix as Marshal Micah Torrance
   Bill Quinn as Sweeney the bartender
   Hope Summers as Hattie Denton the storekeeper
   Patricia Blair as Lou Mallory
   Razor (Lucas)and Blue Boy (Johnny)

Theme Song
"The Rifleman" by Herschel Burke Gilbert

Rifleman Tidbits

Lucas McCain was a widowed rancher living outside of North Fork, New Mexico, and trying to raise his young

son Mark. McCain was an honest, hard-working man who stood up for others against gunslingers, cheats and just plain evil bad guys. Week after week he came to town to confront a desperado. He was a good father to Mark, and taught his son both from the "Good Book" and by example. The stories emphasized the warm love that father and son had for one another. Often the show ended with McCain having to use his rifle to defend the innocent.

McCain was anything but trigger happy, but sometimes this tall, stern-faced man had no choice but to use his gun. McCain's specialty was his skill with his rifle, a specially modified Winchester with a large ring that cocked it as he drew. Supposedly, he could fire within 3/10 of a second. Pretty fast. The sound of his gun was piercing and left a lasting impression. As time passed, Lucas got a bit preachy and was always moralizing about something. Mark was often reduced to finding new and creative ways of saying, "Oh, Pa" and "I'm sorry, Pa."

Chuck Connors had been a professional athlete before becoming an actor. He was a professional basketball player and for a short time played minor and major league baseball. He died in 1992 at the age of 71. Johnny Crawford had begun his acting career as Mouseketeer on the *Mickey Mouse Club.*

Fury

10/15/1955 - 9/3/1966 NBC
Black and White - 30 minutes - 107 episodes
Syndicated as Brave Stallion

Cast
    Peter Graves as Jim Newton
    Bobby Diamond as Joey Newton
    William Fawcett as Pete Wilkie
    Jimmy Baird as Pee Wee (Rodney)Jenkins
    Roger Mobley as Packy Lambert

Theme Song
"Fury" by Ernest Gold

Fury Tidbits

Joey, an orphan, had run afoul of the police after a street fight. He was permitted to live with Jim Newton, the owner of the Broken Wheel Ranch. Newton had recently lost his wife and children in an auto accident. The two needed each other.

The series revolved around Fury, a wild but beautiful black stallion, who was also smart. When Joey arrives at the Broken Wheel Ranch, Fury has never been ridden. Horse and boy eventually become fast friends, and Fury allows Joey to ride him.

Also living on the ranch is Jim Newton's foreman, Pete. Pete has named the horse Fury because he was full of "fire and fury." Each episode had Joey and Fury taking off on new adventures. Often Joey's friends Pee Wee and Packy were involved.

Fury's popularity inspired a number of books by Albert G. Miller with titles like *Fury and the Mustangs* and *Fury Stallion of Broken Wheel Ranch*. *Fury* was a television program that the entire family could enjoy. Filled with adventure and suspense, it taught valuable life lessons. Fury's real name was Beaut and he was owned and trained by Ralph McCutcheon. He received his own fan mail. Peter Graves' brother was James Arness, the star of *Gunsmoke*. Jimmie Baird, who played Pee Wee, was the brother of Mouseketeer Sharon Baird.

American Bandstand

10/7/1957 - 12/30/1989

The most important music show on TV in the 1950s and 1960s was *American Bandstand*, hosted by Dick Clark

graphs. Most of these young singers and groups were at the beginning of their careers, and Clark wisely kept the tapes of their appearances and got full permission to use them in the future. These clips are often seen in rock music retrospectives today, and in some cases, are the only film available of some rock legends (and "one-hit" wonders) early in their careers.

During the remainder of the show Clark played current hits while the studio audience danced to the music. There was also the infamous "rate-a-record" feature ("Umm, it's got a good beat... You can dance to it...I'll give it a 95").

On the afternoon show from 1963 to 1987, kids watched the Regulars every week and copied their clothes, hairstyles and make-up. Among the Regulars were Mike Balara, Walt Gryzelak, Pat Molittieri, Tony Cosmo, Arlene Sullivan, Justine, Frani Giordano, Carolyn Scaldeferri, Betty Romantini, and the Jimenez sisters. Commercials were geared toward the teen audience.

In the fall of 1987 the show was finally cancelled by ABC, but Clark continued production of original episodes for syndication, which were seen on many stations on Saturday afternoons for another year. In the spring of 1989 *Bandstand* surfaced again on the USA cable network, airing at noon on Saturdays. Clark still produced the series but the host was now 26-year-old David Hirsch. This new version lasted less than a year, leaving the air in late 1989. Dick Clark also produced and hosted a number of other prime-time rock music shows, including the Saturday night Dick Clark Show, which ran from 1958 until 1960.

[b.1929], a former DJ with a Philadelphia radio station. The show presented dance competitions for kids and gave both black and white artists the chance to perform their most recent recordings to an audience of millions. Several pop stars, including Fabian, Frankie Avalon, and Connie Francis, owed much of their success to Clark and the show, which had the power to break new artists.

Dick Clark's *American Bandstand* is best known as the networks' longest-running (30 years) afternoon show for teens, but it did have a short run in prime time as well. The show originated live from Philadelphia on 46th and Market Street as a local dance program in 1952, moving to the full ABC network as a Monday-Friday late afternoon entry in August 1957. Its immediate success prompted ABC to give it a brief run on Monday nights that fall. They moved to Hollywood in February 1964.

Clark hosted one or two guest performers whose records were currently on the pop charts. They lip-synched their hits, chatted about their careers, and signed auto-

The Many Loves of Dobie Gillis

10/1959-10/1963, CBS

CAST

Dwayne Hickman as Dobie Gillis
Bob Denver as Maynard G. Krebs
Frank Faylen as Herbert T. Gillis
Florida Friebus asWinifred (Winnie) Gillis
Sheila James as Zelda Gilroy
Thuesday Weld as Thalia Menninger
Darryl Hickman as Davey Gillis
Steve Franken as Chatsworth Osborne, Jr
Warren Beatty as Milton Armitage
Doris Packer as Mrs. Chatsworth Osborne, Sr

Dobie Gillis had three primary interests in life: beautiful women, fancy cars, and money. Unfortunately he was the son of a grocer, which put a certain crimp in his aspirations. Being a typical American teenager, Dobie and his beatnik buddy Maynard did their best to get by with a minimum amount of effort. Dobie had two real nemeses in his life. The first was Zelda Gilroy, who was unceasing in her efforts to marry Dobie, who found her to be smart but annoying and unattractive. Dobie's second nemesis was millionaire Chatsworth Osborne, Jr., a spoiled young man who flaunted his social status and money to snare the attractive girls who eluded Dobie. Maynard G. Krebs, a parody of a beatnik with his goatee and hip slang, became famous for his large ball of tin-foil and his attitude toward work, which he claimed was a dirty word.

When the series premiered in 1959, Dobie had to contend with handsome Milton Armitage for the attention of his favorite girl, the aristocratic Thalia Menninger (played by the young Tuesday Weld). She was interested mostly in acquiring "oodles and oodles" of money, however, and to this end she was always looking to better Dobie's prospects for supporting her in sophisticated style. Dobie was also concerned about his future, and was seen at the beginning and end of each episode in Central City's park next to a statue of The Thinker, assuming the same pose while pondering his fate.

In February 1960, Milton Armitage was replaced by Chatsworth Osborne, Jr., with Doris Packer assuming the role of his snobbish, overbearing mother, essentially the same part she had played as Milton's mother when the series began. In March 1961, Dobie and Maynard enlisted in the army, which didn't work out very well, so they resigned and enrolled in St. Peter Prior Junior College. It was there that they remained, Maynard still fighting the system in his nonconformist way and his "good buddy" Dobie chasing women and trying to find himself, for the last two seasons the show was on the air.

My Little Margie

6/16/1952 - 8/24/1955 CBS (30 min.)

CAST:
  Don Hayden as Freddie Wilson
  Gale Storm as Margaret 'Margie' Albright
  Hillary Brooke as Roberta Townsend
  Willie Best as Charlie
  Gertrude Hoffman as Mrs. Odetts
  Charles Farrell as Vernon 'Vern' Albright
        [former silent screen star]
  Clarence Kolb as George Honeywell
  Diane Fauntelle as Regular Performer
  George Meader as Mr. Todd

My Little Margie was the story of Margie Albright, the vivacious, irrepressible, 21-year-old daughter of Vernon Albright, a widowed executive at the investment-counseling firm of Honeywell & Todd. The Albrights resided in a Fifth Avenue apartment in New York.

Margie was always trying to help her father get a client, avoid a designing woman, or trying to get him to act his age as she felt he should. Margie's elaborate plans almost always included a disguise of some sort. She masqueraded as everything from a male opera singer to Vern's mother to her own, non-existent sister to the Albright's equally non-existent maid. Usually helping with her schemes were the spunky Mrs. Odetts, the Albright's aged neighbor, and Freddie Wilson, Margie's ardent boyfriend, whom Vern disliked intently. Other characters in the mix were Mr. Honeywell, Vern's exasperated boss;

Roberta, Vern's girlfriend; and Charlie, the elevator operator in the Albright's apartment building.

In 1952, the TV series *My Little Margie* became a radio series, which ran concurrently with the TV series. Episodes were Radioactive Margie, Margie Sings Opera, Margie's Sister Sally, Margie Plays Detective, The Blonde Margie, Margie's Career, Conservative Margie, Hillbilly Margie, Homely Margie, My Little Bookie, Go North, Young Girl, Margie the Writer, Delinquent Margie, Margie's Man proof Lipstick and Margie Baby-sits

In the last episode, Margie helps the daughter of one of Vern's clients elope against her father's wishes. Vern thinks it is Margie who has eloped.

The Real McCoys

10/3/1957 - 9/22/1963

CAST
  Walter Brennan as Grandpa Amos McCoy
  Richard Crenna as Luke McCoy
  Kathy Nolan as Kate McCoy
  Lydia Reed as 'Aunt' Hassie
  Michael Winkleman as Little Luke
  Tony Martinez as Pepino Garcia

Andy Clyde as George MacMichael
Madge Blake as FIora MacMichael
Betty Garde as Aggie Larkin
Janet De Gore as Louise Howard
Butch Patrick as Greg Howard
Joan Blondell as Winifred Jordan

When this rural comedy was first proposed to the networks by the writers, the experts said it would never work. Okay for the sticks, maybe, but no good for city viewers. NBC finally turned the series down cold. Walter Brennan wanted nothing to do with it. But the Pincus brothers persevered. Brennan was finally won over, financing was obtained from Danny Thomas Productions, and a spot was found. *The Real McCoys* became one of the biggest hits on TV for the next six years; it started a major trend toward rural comedy shows which lasted through the 1960s. This was the inspiration for *The Andy Griffith Show, Beverly Hillbillies, Petticoat Junction, Green Acres*, and several others.

The premise was simple: a happy-go-lucky West Virginia mountain family picks up stakes and moves to a ranch in California's San Fernando Valley. Center of the action, and undisputed star of the show, was Grandpa, a porch-rockin', gol-darnin', consarnin' old codger with a wheezy voice who liked to meddle in practically everybody's affairs, neighbors and kin alike.

Three-time Academy Award-winner Walter Brennan (who was 63 when the series began) played the role to perfection. The cantankerous but lovable Grandpa Amos McCoy walked with bent elbows, jumping shoulders, and a hitch in his step—a gait Brennan had perfected decades earlier in *To Have and Have Not*. He also made a few recordings, the most popular being "Old Rivers" in 1962. His kin were grandson Luke and his new bride, Kate; Luke's teenage sister, "Aunt" Hassie; and Luke's 11-year-old brother, Little Luke (their parents were deceased). Completing the regular cast were Pepino, the musically inclined farm hand, and George MacMichael, their argumentative neighbor. George's spinster sister Flora had eyes for Grandpa, but she never did snare him.

In 1962, when the series moved to CBS, Luke became a widower and many of the plots began to revolve around Grandpa's attempts to match him up with a new wife. The series ended in 1963. CBS aired reruns with the title shortened to The McCoys, from 1962 to 1966 on weekday mornings.

Lassie

9/1/1954 - 9/1/1974 CBS (30 min.)

CAST:
Tommy Rettig as Jeff Miller
Cloris Leachman as Ruth Martin
June Lockhart as Ruth Martin
Arthur Space as Doc Weaver
George Chandler as Uncle Petrie Martin
Florence Lake as Jennie

Jon Provost as Timmy Martin
Jan Clayton as Ellen Miller
Andy Clyde as Cully Wilson
Donald Keeler as Sylvester "Porky" Brockway
Sue Lambert as Sherry Boucher
Hugh Reilly as Paul Martin
George Cleveland as Grandpa Miller
John Sheppod as Paul Martin
Robert Bray as Corey Stuart, Forest Ranger
Paul Maxey as Matt Brockway

Lassie was a remarkably brave, loyal and intelligent collie. Families fell in love with the dog, who was always willing to help and protect his masters. The original story was about a young boy and his companion collie. Jeff Miller lived on a small farm near Calverton with his widowed mother and grandfather. Some may remember the antics of Jeff and his friend Porky who wore a "little rascals" hat and called out a special code of Eee-ock-eee!

By the spring of 1957 a runaway orphan named Timmy had joined the Miller family household. That fall, Grandpa died and the family moved to the city. Lassie and Timmy stayed behind and remained in the care of the Martins, the neighbors who were childless. The show became the Weekly Adventures of Timmy and Lassie. In 1968 Lassie and the Adventures with Ranger Corey began. The Lassie story originated in *Lassie Come Home*, a best-selling novel which later became a movie and radio series.

First episode:

Lassie is left to Jeff in a will after her previous owner dies. The hired hand is found trying to steal the $2000 cash the old man had hidden in the old home. The hired hand locks Lassie and Jeff up in the old house and tries to escape with the money. Lassie chases down the crook and, with the help of a neighbor, regains the cash. Lassie makes her decision to stay with her new family.

Last episode:

Lassie tracks down the Baker calf, on the loose and endangered by predators.

Chapter 3
WHAT WE WORE

Teenage Fashions in the 1950s

During the 50s teenage girls never wore slacks or jeans in school, but once classes were over they often took on the uniform of turned-up jeans and a white shirt "borrowed" from their dads or big brothers. The shirt was worn with the tails hanging out and sometimes tied in front. The outfit was completed with bobby sox and loafers or saddle shoes. For awhile the loafers were called penny loafers because it was popular to slip a penny into the front slit. This look was comfortable and within the means of almost everyone.

The preppy look emerged in the early Fifties as a full skirt supported by several crinolines or even a hoop that would emphasize a tiny waist. The more crinolines the better. The poodle skirt--a felt circle skirt with poodle appliqué made of pom-poms and yarn—had become popular by the mid-fifties, and the poodle itself became somewhat of an icon, appearing on sweaters and in jewelry. The skirts were often worn with a cinched belt. Flats, ballerina shoes and even white bucks were the preferred footwear among young girls.

The feminine greaser look or "tough" image was beginning to emerge with the appearance of movies like Rebel without a Cause, in which the women wore heavy make-up and tight sweaters over a tight bra.

Bermuda shorts were hugely popular in the 1950's and 60's. Some girls wore short shorts. This escalated the debate among school administrators that continued until dress codes began to appear in junior and senior high schools across the nation. Many schools, even parochial ones, began to measure a girl's skirt length. A student might be sent home for wearing a skirt that was too short, or for wearing culottes. Girls were not allowed to wear pants in school until the 1970's.

Those who preferred to wear longer shorts could wear Capri pants that reached mid-calf. Capri's were also called "pedal pushers" because they had no cuffs, so that you could wear them while riding a bicycle without fear they would catch in the chain. The song "Short Shorts" by the Royal Teens and Carl Perkin's "Pink Pedal Pushers" could be heard on juke boxes across the nation. Both these songs made the charts in 1958.

Growing up in the Sixties

Anyone who grew up during the sixties will remember the cliques. The smart kids had their group. Then there was the "in" or cool group, who typically wore expensive clothes and hung out at special places before and after school. Last of all, there was the greaser-type group who had greasy hair and wore black

things. The boys wore letter jackets, Gant shirts, wheat-colored jeans and saddle shoes that were black and white or cordovan. I remember my boyfriend wearing white saddle shoes with his suit as he walked down the aisle at ninth grade graduation. The shoes stuck out like a sore thumb.

Junior High

In the summertime, we made our own outfits. We all had the same pattern that we passed around, but the colors were different and sometimes the fabric. These were short-sleeved crop tops or v-necked vests with matching Bermuda shorts. Our families didn't have extra money, so we were very thrifty. Lee Ann could sew but she had to have help reading the pattern because the instructions were complicated. Cotton checks came in different colors and mine was bottle green. Lee Ann's was red checked and Roxanne's was bright blue.

In junior high, we wore pleated wool skirts with matching cardigan sweaters and knee highs. I wonder if my sister knew that I borrowed her outfits quite often and rolled up the skirts to make them fit. Blouses were very popular—for example the Nothing blouse, the Ben Casey shirt and the Patriot-style blouse that was reminiscent of those worn during the Revolutionary War, with ruffles at the neck and sleeve. Even the guys wore them. British bands that started wearing them suddenly became popular. Cha-cha blouses had layers of ruffles all the way down the front and were buttoned up in back. Usually they came in white, but I made mine out of fabric with a pink-flowered print. Angel blouses came in during the

leather. The greaser girls would tease up their hair rather than comb it down.

I was crushed because I was not in any of these groups, though I tried hard to be. But my position as an outsider proved to be a blessing, as I was able to have friends from each group and even friends that were not in any group. The smart group was too square and dull for me, and I was not intellectual enough for them anyway. I was too smart to be in the "in group," although this was the group I tried to be in. I wanted to be popular and smart, but that didn't seem to be an option at the time. I was insecure so it was easy to conform. We all dressed alike and the girls wore their wool sweaters and matching short pleated skirts with knee-high socks. Madras plaid was popular. The colors everyone wore were navy blue, cranberry, cordovan and hunter green. We all had our Roger Van "S" purses, which cost about $22. That was a lot of money for me considering I only made $17 a week, but I would rather have died than go without these

summer of 1960. They were flared out at the bodice and had a lace hem at the waist. Dickies were popular, too. Angora sweaters, popular during the Fifties, were often stored in the refrigerator to keep shedding to a minimum.

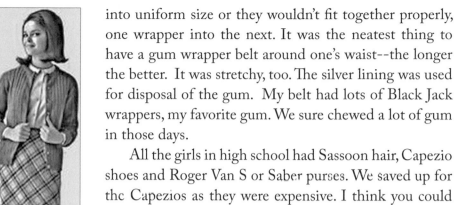

By the early '60s these sweaters were mixed with mink, rabbit, and other furs that still shed some but looked fabulous and didn't wear out as easily as the ones from the earlier time. In ladies' tops or blouses, the turtleneck or polo neck sweater was common, especially under a collarless jacket.

Wool plaid jumpers and skirts were popular, as well as shifts, sack dresses, shirtwaists and straight skirts. Peacoats came in loden green or navy blue, and tie blouses made of crepe were worn together with A line skirts.

I will always remember sneaking to put on white lipstick and rolling up my skirt (just an inch or two) after my sister went to school in the morning. When I was in high school, all of the girls wore their hair in a flip.

I remember making my own gum-wrapper belt. After chewing the gum, I would fold the wrappers together in a way that was like weaving. They had to be folded into uniform size or they wouldn't fit together properly, one wrapper into the next. It was the neatest thing to have a gum wrapper belt around one's waist--the longer the better. It was stretchy, too. The silver lining was used for disposal of the gum. My belt had lots of Black Jack wrappers, my favorite gum. We sure chewed a lot of gum in those days.

All the girls in high school had Sassoon hair, Capezio shoes and Roger Van S or Saber purses. We saved up for the Capezios as they were expensive. I think you could only get them at Dayton's. Bobby Brook's plaid skirts were great, too. Remember Earth Shoes? The theory was that walking in them gave the same affect as walking on a sandy beach [the heel was lower than the rest of the foot]. Some people developed shin splints while trying to get used to them. Earth Shoes came with a cool burlap sack that we put our prized possessions in and carried around. It was common to walk funny in these shoes to make a heel impression look lower in the sand to prove the Earth Shoe's claim was true.

Fashion:1950's American Bandstand Sets the Standards

There was a dress code on American Bandstand. They didn't want kids on it looking like James Dean or Marlon Brando. But there was plenty of variation outside of that. Millions of teenage viewers watched the show and copied what they saw.

Guys wore suits or sport jackets with dress slacks and mandatory, conservative ties. Open-necked shirts were still many years ahead. Gray flannel, confetti tweeds or intricate cross-hatched tweed in deep navy or black were popular for jacket styles. The pants, a carryover from the Zoot suit of the Swing era, were baggy and pleated, and worn with wing tips, oxfords or penny loafers. The common haircut for guys was the slicked back DA look which was a ducktail in the back, sides short, and a Bryl-creamed pompadour in the front.

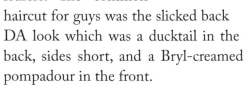

The ladies wore their hair in a short Pixie or teased it up in a bubble hair-do. Also flips, braids and pony or pig tails were popular. Barrettes and bobby pins flowed in abundance and bows and headbands became all the rage once the kids on Bandstand started wearing them. Perky and neat, a ponytail could spare a girl the nightly chore of rolling up her hair. Girls wore duck tails, too.

A girl's fashion included dresses that had small collars and pleated skirts. Whether the skirt was pencil slim or outrageously full and rounded-out by petticoats, it fell well below the knee. There were green and blue watchplaids and big black and white window-pane plaids.

White blouses worn with dark skirts were stylishly classic. Poodle Skirts swung nicely at a girl's knees when she danced with her guy during the Spotlight dance.

By 1958 both circle skirts and crinolines were on the way out. Full and gathered skirts replaced circle skirts, though they still had lots of crinolines. Nineteen fifty-seven and fifty-eight saw a huge return to chemises and shifts from the 1920s. Peter Pan collars worn beneath sweaters, surprisingly, were merely white school uniform collars. Kids wrote in asking, "Hey, where can I get me one of those Philadelphia collars?"

Style Setters

High-school girls dressed alike. Nothing would do but a dress or skirt paired with a neat, close-fitting blouse, sweater, or even cooler, a sweater set with a string of pearls around the neck. The cool girl wore flats, penny loafers, or well-scuffed saddle shoes with bobby socks. Local style governed whether to cuff them or not, but one dictum was universal: they had to be white. Accessories were broaches, circle pins or wearable toys like mink dogs on a chain. Charm bracelets were the latest thing to fill the dresser drawers of most teenaged girls, along with basket pocketbooks and cat's eye glasses with sequins and rhinestones on the rims.

Pullover sweaters were accessorized with detachable collars. An initial pin individualized a girl's outfit. Long-sleeved, button-up sweaters came in plain or ribbed neck and were often beaded or appliquéd. Sweaters were wool or acrylic knit, but cashmere gave status. Sweaters and collars were probably the biggest fashion trends for girls during the mid 50's. Angora sweaters, cotton blends and new synthetic materials were worn in solid or patterned cardigans that were crew- or v-necked. Fur collars, especially rabbit fur, were added as adornment. Velvet and satin made up most trim, along with leopard collars with matching belts.

To dress for the holidays or for parties, girls would wear fancy ball gowns with nylons and high-heeled pumps. It was the innocent age of tulle party dresses padded with multiple crinoline petticoats underneath. Strapless, fitted eveningwear was worn with a heart-shaped over-bodice of opaque silk or nylon. Some of these gowns were long-sleeved. On Prom night, evening gowns were pastel nylon tulle, usually bedecked with yards of tulle trims, ruffles and velvet bows. A black satin or velvet bodice with white chiffon skirt was hugely popular. Brocades, taffeta, nylon net, and chiffon were common materials and the effect of overlaying contrasting sheer chiffon or net over a flesh-colored dress was all the rage. Evening colors were both subtle and bold, as peacock blues and hot pinks became acceptable. Diamond tiaras were trendy and worn by most girls.

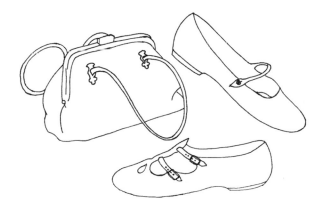

Fashion in the 1960's

Men's casual shirts were often plaid and buttoned down the front, while knee-length dresses were worn by the women. By the mid-decade, miniskirts or hot pants, often worn with go-go boots, exposed a good deal of a woman's legs. Menswear changed to bright colors; double-breasted sports jackets, polyester pants with Nehru jackets and turtlenecks were in vogue.

By 1964, the hemlines started to creep up. Nineteen sixty-six was the year of the mini-skirt! The brainchild of designer Mary Quant, anybody who had the body to pull it off was wearing one within the year. Many hemlines that were 4-5 inches above the knee in New York, were 7-8 inches above the knee in London! Skirts were often paired with a matching sweater and tights for that uniform look. Nineteen sixty-five and six also saw the mini-coat, which was perfectly straight and virtually shapeless. By 1967, capes had become popular. Coatdresses from the 1950s in lightweight wools became popular again. The sleeve, which was usually ¾ length, was pushed partway up the arm for a Jackie O look. Sleeveless tops did not come into popularity until the mid-1960's.

Baldies and Greasers

The Baldies of the Sixties were boys with very short crew cuts, wearing Florsheim steel-toed wingtips, V-neck cashmere sweaters, and khaki pants pulled high up the waist. Yellow, button-down oxford shirts and madras were popular; the most prestigious brand was Gant, which was renowned for the small loop on the back pleat.

mals, who supposedly filed their teeth to a point, but no one ever saw any of these guys.

The greaser look was tougher and flashier and smacked of rebellious, if not outright juvenile delinquency behavior. Greasers followed the black leather and denim-jeans look set by Marlon Brando in *The Wild One* and James Dean in *Rebel Without a Cause* (later emulated, and virtually parodied, in the 1978 film called *Grease*). Greasers raced about town on motorbikes and were considered outrageous. They wore pegged pants or cuffed tight black jeans, and boots. They rolled up the sleeves of their T-shirts to show off their biceps and made a hand pocket in the arm for stashing a pack of cigarettes. The hallmark greaser hair style was the ducktail, or DA. Many high schools were so convinced by the DA's dangerous influence that some banned it. Achieving a well-sculpted ducktail called for Vaseline or a heavy dose of hair preparation like Wildroot Cream Oil, Brylcream or Vitalis. A comb was kept ready for sweeping back stray locks.

In the popular TV show *77 Sunset Strip*, which ran from 1958 to 1964, a hip, young parking lot attendant named Gerald Lloyd Kookson III, more popularly known as "Kookie" was continually running a comb through his greasy locks. This habit inspired the hit single "Kookie, Kookie (Lend Me Your Comb)" in which a girl (Connie Stevens) keeps asking Kookie to put down his comb so she can get romantic.

The colors were navy blue, burgundy and bottle green. Letter jackets, short haircuts and dessert boots were also part of this style, which would later evolve into the preppy or rich-kid style. Baldies were known for neatness in grooming.

The fabled mid-Sixty Baldies vs. Greasers gang turf battles in the Twin Cities were basically a "class" thing with the well-dressed, modish Baldies at odds with the more working-class, white T-shirt and levis-clad Greasers. Rumors abounded concerning gangs like The Ani-

Fashion Memories from the 50s

Nancy O'Dette

In the 50s, my friends and I wore pink ranch pants. They were tightly fitted, styled like saddle pants, and were made out of denim or wool. They came in black and pastels and had two little pockets in front with a pearl snap on them. We wore them everywhere and thought they were so cool. Hairstyles that were popular were the pixie, ponytail and finger curls made with clips. We wore a stiff blouse with silk scarf tied around the neck or a short-sleeved sweater with separate velvet or felt collar that attached. Full skirts with crinolines or hoop skirts were worn by everyone and were cinched with an eight-inch belt made with a rubber gold hook. We would sugar starch the crinolines on hoops and wear four or five of them at once. On a Thursday night we would dip them in sugar and lay them out on the bedroom floor. On Saturday, when we put them on, our legs beneath would become sticky from sugar. We also wore bib jumpers made of mint green cotton. For shoes, we wore saddle shoes or gray wedgies. The guys wore plaid shirts and loose kaki pants. Hair for guys was a flat top with fenders, which was a crew cut on top and ducktail in the back.

Sewing and Home Ec.

I first took sewing in the seventh grade at Northeast Junior High. Mind you, I was a real geeky teenager. I couldn't seem to get ready in the morning in time to catch the school bus that was four blocks away. We didn't have a car in those days, and when I missed the bus I had to try and catch a city bus that ran occasionally or miss school altogether. My hair was always frizzed and sticking out in every which direction and my catalog order clothes didn't fit just right. Need I say I was confused and missed the city bus half the time? I missed a lot of school that year.

Mrs. Ferrell was our Home Ec sewing teacher. She was tall, thin and had short cropped hair that made her look like a drill sergeant. I'm not sure why I was so resistant to her; I wasn't that way with any of my other teachers. I guess I wasn't used to the dictator type and rebelled every chance I got. She had no patience in trying to teach me how to sew.

The sewing machines we used in class were electric with a pedal on the floor. I couldn't seem to guide the fabric and push the foot pedal at the same time. [I had the same trouble in learning to drive.] The machine went too fast, which rattled me up. At home I had used a treadle machine to sew on occasionally, and it had a slow steady pace and was easy to control.

Mrs. Ferrell insisted that I keep sewing even though it made me crazy. I should have practiced on a scrap of material more to get used to the machine and learn to control the pace, but we only had so much time in class. (Time in general in those days was my enemy.)

Our first project was a simple blouse with no sleeves or collar. I bought myself five yards of fabric, one yard of lavender floral for the blouse and four yards of white polished cotton for the skirt. I don't know what I was thinking because I never wore white skirts. I had a pattern and was anxious to prove that I could be a woman who could sew. This proved to be an expensive learning experience. After I cut out my creation, pre-washed the fabric and stay-stitched all the seams, I finally got to sew on it. I only had to rip out my stitching on the blouse a few times, but the skirt was another story. I didn't understand that the pins had to go inside of the pattern

lines. I kept putting them on the cutting line with the tips sticking out over the edge. I learned that you couldn't cut through pins, so I had to take them all out and do it again. It was not a good-looking blouse at the end. By the time I got to the gathered skirt part, I was in trouble. White, polished cotton was the worst for showing every mistake.

When I finally finished the project, the fabric might just as well have been burlap, with all the uneven stitches in it and so many holes torn from the many times I had ripped out the stitching. I would never have worn that outfit anywhere. I ripped the gathers out at least ten times. To this day, if I see one of those seam rippers I get a sinking feeling. The rotary marking tool and waxy paper drove me nuts, too. It slipped all over the place and the lines didn't trace to where they should have been. Mrs. Ferrell gave me an F for the project. I suppose it was partly because of my attitude. It was the only F I had ever received in school and had to go to summer school to try and learn the skill. The next year, I received straight A's in sewing and even helped others with their projects. The difference was the teacher—though I suppose I had also learned a few things by ripping out those seams so many times .

For the next quarter, I had Cooking. This teacher was very sweet, but I didn't do well in her class either. We made food together as a group. The dishes were supposed to be healthy and easy to make, but some of them were disgusting, especially since they probably weren't made correctly. I remember making carrot and raisin salad and egg custard with caramel on the bottom. My caramel turned out rock hard. My grade in that class was a C+.

Fashion Sewing in the 1960s

Fashion sewing was very popular during the early sixties and a major subject in secondary schools in the United States. Female pupils often had at least two sessions of dressmaking and needlecrafts per week. Most young girls were expected to leave school with good sewing skills. Many were easily able to make dresses, blouses and skirts.

For most girls, creative subjects were effectively squeezed out by the Junior and Senior High curriculum.

Most academic girls felt obliged to opt for qualifications that would help them get jobs or go to college.

Even so, night classes abounded. Dressmaking was very popular and most women could manage to make a dress if they attended ten sessions. Once they had the rudimentary skill of using a sewing machine and pattern cutting, many continued to learn by teaching themselves through pattern directions. In the 1960s, instructions in sewing patterns were very detailed and far superior to patterns available today. Patterns often contained four or five instruction sheets, but the difference between them was that those sheets would be in English or English and French. Now the instructions come in many languages but some of the actual construction details have been omitted.

Night class projects began with an apron and simple blouse. Students graduated into making gathered skirts and dresses. They were instructed on how to pick out fabric, lay out a pattern, make darts, gathers, waist bands, sleeves, collars, and learn the basics of hemming.

Amluxen's and Learning to Sew

Joannie Moses

Amluxen's had the most gorgeous fabrics from around the world. Many were from Europe, Pakistan and India. They also had buttons and trims that you couldn't find anywhere else. I bought blue mohair fabric for $33 a yard in 1963. My teacher was afraid to cut it and wouldn't okay my pattern layout. She said my mother needed to look at it. She knew my mother was a seamstress.

I also bought embroidered linen that I still have today. These fabrics were hard to come by. The trims were fabulous and you could buy tricot for sewing lingerie. There was a time when making your own lingerie was very popular and you could get discounted fabric at Munsingwear. I made a coatdress in 1964 with bound buttonholes made by hand. Sewing was huge in the six-

ties and everyone did it. Quite a few stores had fabric with rows and rows of cabinets filled with patterns. Fashion history can often be traced very accurately by looking at old sewing patterns. McCalls, Butterick, Vogue, and Simplicity patterns were the most common. People also did all kinds of needlework such as embroidering, knitting, crocheting and smocking. Those were great ways to pass the time. People used to save buttons and use them again.

In Junior high you had to have at least one year of Home Ec, which included cooking, sewing, childcare, laundry, crafts and knitting. Our first sewing project was an apron. For sewing we used the Bishop method, which was a certain way of putting together clothes. You sewed all the darts first before putting the garment together. We used interfacing, tracing wheels, chalk, and thread dipped in beeswax. We had to stay-stitch everything to prevent stretching and pink all the seams to prevent raveling.

My Sewing Machine

My mother bought me a Sears Kenmore sewing machine in 1966 as a graduation present. She bought it on the installment plan. Lay-by was a great way to purchase things long before credit cards

were common. How exciting it was to pick up your item after paying weekly and sometimes for several months. The total cost was $67. It had a nice walnut cabinet. I don't think it was one of the top models, but it has lasted to this day. I started making clothes in my teen years. I made all of the dresses that I wore on my honeymoon. I would buy one pattern and make it again and again in different versions, fabrics and colors. Midnight often found me whipping up something for a special occasion. Having a yen for pretty clothes might have been too much of a good thing, but it made me learn the value of a dollar and how to make the most out of a small amount. It also taught me how to use my creativity, ingenuity and skill.

Newspaper Patterns

A popular feature in hundreds of newspapers in the 50's and 60's was the sale of sewing patterns. Sometimes they were featured next to a recipe for creamed turkey or ham. Pattern layouts included aprons, housedresses, baby clothes, children's play clothes and home decor items.

They sometimes showcased popular pattern items like appliance covers. Apron patterns would occasionally come with an iron-on transfer to be applied and embroidered on after the sewing was done. These were added incentives to buy them.

Seasonal items were also a favorite. Halloween costumes and Christmas crafts, which included crochet, tatting and embroidery patterns, were popular. These pattern offers were a boon to rural woman and to those who didn't drive. And all for just thirty cents! The ad requested payment in the form of coins and it was acceptable to tape them to a piece of cardboard or paper and send them in the mail.

Prom was a Special Night

Prom was the most glamorous event of the year. It was a time when matching sweaters, skirts and knee-highs were shed and teenagers tried to be sophisticated adults. Boys dressed in white dinner jackets and boutonnières and girls wore strapless dresses made with floaty skirts of satin, taffeta or voile. It was customary for the boy to present his date with a corsage when he arrived at her house. This custom had a great deal of importance. It was all about prestige and proof of affection. The best flowers were roses and orchids. The flowers were supposed to coordinate with the girl's dress color, but sometimes didn't.

The dance floor was filled with the scent of English Leather, Brut and Canoe, the most popular colognes for guys at the time. For girls it was Tabu, Tigress, Yardley or Bonne Bell cologne. Pearls or rhinestone necklaces, bracelets and earrings were favorites among girls for a formal evening and often a girl's heels were dyed to match her dress. Good dancers were envied.

At some time during the night the couple waited in line patiently and posed for the ritual photograph. Both parties had to display prom-night manners. There was always the interest of who was with whom. And the highlight of the evening was the tender slow dance with your supposed "sweetie." Every Prom had a theme that was carried out in the invitations and décor.

Although I didn't go to my prom, I helped decorate the gym with black paper butterflies that had brightly colored cellophane inserts for the wings and hung from the ceiling. If you put them near the light the wings looked like stained glass. Tissue paper flowers made of turquoise, yellow and hot pink made the gym come alive. Palm trees were of painted cardboard. A white picket fence arbor with a bridge across a stream and a real water fountain added just the right touch. All the same, it was hard to transform an empty gymnasium that had hardwood floors with painted lines and basketball hoops into something special. Elusive Butterfly was the theme named after the most popular song of that year (1967).

Going to my future husband's prom was kind of strange because I didn't know anyone else. He went to an all-boys school and wasn't really into the prom thing, so I knew he took me because I wanted to go. I borrowed a dress from my friend Roxanne and wore pettipants underneath and pale white lipstick. On Prom night, I had my hair done at Donaldson's where I worked at the

Betty and Roger Kieley, 1961

downstairs Café. They did it up in Grecian curls and the hairdresser thought it looked so great that I should have my picture taken for free. I thought it looked like I had a bushel basket on my head, so I took it down when I got home and styled it myself. I still have the picture. I don't know what I was thinking when I took it down. I guess I was just nervous and wanted it to look perfect. I wished I could have relaxed and had a good time. We ate at Howard Wong's afterward where we passed around silver serving dishes, which was different than what I was used to at restaurants. We doubled with a friend of his from school and drove in his souped up red 1957 Chevy.

Getting Ready for Prom

These were the places to go for getting ready for Prom night. Some exclusive hair salons downtown were the Golden Door, the Golden Razor and Adam and Eve. Bridal Shops downtown were Rush's, Barbara Bridal, Schaffer's and the Bridal Shop. The best place to have your shoes dyed to match your dress was Chandler's Shoe Store.

Some of the best local restaurants for eating after the Prom were: Murrays, the Rainbow Cafe on Lake Street, Charlie's Cafe Exceptional, the Waikiki room at the Nicollet Hotel, Little Jacks, Jacks, McCarthy's in Golden Valley and Howard Wong's on 494.

Crinolines

In the 1950's, the "New Look" for Christian Dior featured small waists that were accentuated by full skirts. The skirts were supported by twenty-five yards of fabric. Although crinolines were an expected foundation for a net formal, Dior's style went beyond the elegant evening gown and became a necessity for the everyday dress of the teenage girl.

Crinolines were petticoats made from netting or paper nylon. They were gathered in stiffly starched tiers to provide the lift needed to flare out a young girl's skirts. Lingerie departments added space to the garment section by offering a huge assortment of colors to choose from. The "Petti Pretty" was a can-can version of nylon net that came in gay rainbow fluff. It sold for $2.99 in 1955. Often these were of three tiers and came in powdery pastels. For added embellishment, the white net petticoat was sometimes bordered at the bottom by a band of multi-colored embroidery.

In 1956, if you were a sixteen year old girl, you'd be wearing three starched crinolines beneath your new full skirt. Proper manners meant you would carefully tuck your skirt beneath you when you sat down. Then, you'd put your hands over your knees to keep the skirt from flying up toward the ceiling and revealing your underwear. Sometimes the skirt would spring up on both sides and hit the person next to you in the face.

Teenagers would repeatedly wash their crinolines by swishing them around in sugar water in the bathtub and wringing them out gently, then laying them to dry over opened umbrellas in the basement.

One solution for a limp crinoline was simply to add a new hoop petticoat. The ribbons of this creation were laced with stiff nylon "bones," so it would never wear out! And there was no question as to which of her petticoats a young woman would give up for this new one. She would simply add the new hoop petticoat to the others, wearing it as a third layer, and keeping the other crinolines on top to smooth over the "bones."

Madras

Everyone wore Madras in the 1960's. The amazing new material was carefree permanent press, but its main attraction was that when it was washed, the colors would "bleed." It was the hottest

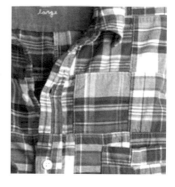

fashion of high school. The garment had to be washed in cold water to keep "bleeding" to a minimum. Gant shirts were for guys and blouses for girls. There were also wrap-around skirts, shorts and jackets made out of madras. Some girls even had matching purses.

Ben Casey shirt/blouse

The Ben Casey shirt/blouse was modeled after the tunic worn by the popular TV doctor, Ben Casey (played by Vince Edwards) whose show was seen on ABC Monday nights from 1961 to 1966. Viewers loved the opening sequence, during which symbols for man, woman, birth, death and infinity were portentiously drawn on the screen. Ben Casey was a surly surgeon, but his animal magnetism made him a star, though unlike his ratings-rival Dr. Kildare, Ben Casey occasionally lost a patient.

Charm Bracelets

Charm bracelets became extremely popular among women during the 1950's and the 1960's. The various charms, selected and purchased individually, could become a chronicle of a young woman's life, encapsulating her loves, interests, travels, and experiences. These objects told her individual story and also preserved it for future generations.

The end of World War II saw the explosion of charm jewelry as soldiers returned to the United States from Europe and the Pacific islands with handmade trinkets for their sweethearts, fashioned by native craftsmen out of small bits of metal into replicas of items natural to the locale. Enterprising jewelers in the United States soon picked up on the trend to create charms for all occasions.

By the 1950's, the charm bracelet was a must-have accessory for girls and women. Major rites of passage, such as a sixteenth-birthday celebration, graduation, wedding, vacation, or the birth of a child, were all recorded by adding links to the bracelet. The first charm a young girl received might be a ballerina or flower. Her teenage years may see the addition of a love-token from a sweetheart, a souvenir from a school trip or a jeweled mortar board at graduation. Then came charms com-

memorating her engagement, wedding, first home, and children.

Perhaps a tiny pearl typewriter would signify that she enjoyed the independence of having a job outside of the home. Jeweled representations of her interests and hobbies were often received as gifts and added to her bracelet. Other charms were simply for beauty. In contrast to the flat charms of modern times, vintage charms were three-dimensional, highly detailed, and often jeweled. They were works of art in their own right.

The charm bracelet began to disappear from the fashion scene by the early 1970s. Disco was in, gold chains became the new status symbol, and charms were out. But in the mid-1980's, charms reappeared and continued for years to be worn by ladies of all ages.

Hot Pants

During their heyday, Hot Pants were not just an article of ordinary ho-hum sportswear, but a brandnew, outrageous style that was higher cut, tighter, and altogether skimpier than ever! No longer fashioned of sturdy denim and broadcloth, these were made of flashier stuff such as mink, monkey fur, silk, satin, calfskin, chiffon and cut velvet. The accepted generic term sounded like an adolescent joke, but short shorts were serious business and women in major European and U.S. cities were risking their fashion reputations, and also running a risk of frostbite, to wear them.

Some credited the craze to anti-midi and pro-leg passion. Broadtail mink shorts were priced as high as $200. In Paris, mini-shorts were an every night disco affair. They were particularly suited for dancing because they allowed for more freedom of movement. Some of the more popular versions included Valentino's All-Sequined variety.

The boutique of Yves St. Laurent in Los Angeles sold out every shipment that came in. The favorite was a slightly flared, black velvet number selling at $60. Satin and crepe versions were hardly less popular at $50. Actress Ursula Andress dined out in her bronze velvet shorts while Raquel Welch owned a special pair of white matte jersey. Manhattan stores and boutiques could hardly match supply to demand. Jackie Onassis stocked up on Ralston's shorties for yacht wear, and career girls like fabric-coordinator Jacquie Nelson were granted permission to wear their knit shorts to work.

Hot Pants came in every fabric and color imaginable—tie-dyed print, zig zag, multicolored, psychedelic, velvet, wool, dotted-Swiss, shorts-and-sweater sets, zippered, cuffed… you name it!

Go Go Boots

Go Go Boots were the brain-child of a Parisian designer named Andre Courreges. His collection introduced white dresses with hems three inches above the knee coupled with white mid-calf boots called "kid boots." That year his collection over-shadowed more sea-soned designers such as Coco Chanel. In 1965, Nancy Sinatra topped the music charts with her smash hit, "These Boots Were Made for Walking." The record sold almost four mil-lion copies and she will

be forever remembered as the poster child for go-go boots. By the spring of 1965, go-go boots had begun to fall out of fashion as designers showed shorter skirts and higher boots.

Go-Go dancers were mini-skirted club-goers who made a splash at such places as Whisky A Go-Go, a West Hollywood nightclub. This celebrated club was among the first to have dancers performing in elevated cages and wearing Go-Go boots. Go-Go is said to derive from a French phrase meaning "in abundance galore." In Paris, there was one such disco club that bore the same name. Goldie Hawn helped to bring the Go-Go dancer into the cultural mainstream on the comedy TV show Laugh In. Though rock-and-roll variety shows such as Hullaballo and Shindig also featured Go-Go dancers behind many of the acts.

Mohair Sweaters

In 1963 and 1964, the big fad was Mohair sweaters. These oversized, fluffy sweaters came in pullover and cardigan styles and an array of colors ranging from baby blue and baby pink to baby lilac, baby or-ange, baby yellow and baby red. Every girl had to have more than one! Mohair was expensive, how-ever, so friends often bought one and shared it with each other. Some wore Angora sweaters and used the threads to wrap around the back of their boyfriend's class ring, which would otherwise be too big to stay on their finger.

Mohair comes from the Angora goat. The word Mohair is a Turkish word meaning the 'best selected fleece.' It was known in Biblical times, and the cur-tains on the Hebrew Tabernacle were woven from the snow white fleece of the goat (Ex.26:7). In later years, the animal became restricted to the Turkish province of Angora [which is now Ankara] and its fleece was highly sought after making clothes for the Sultan. Prized as one of the world's most luxurious natural fibers, mohair is hollow and therefore brings warmth, but is very lightweight.

Growing Mohair is no easy task. The Angora goat is a graceful, delicate animal, but is susceptable to disease in wet or dry conditions. Dedicated Angora farmers have to protect their flocks from predators such as baboons, jackals and coyotes that will chase a young Angora goat to death, and they must also work to preserve the purity of the breed.

Empire-Waist Dresses

A type of dress or top where the waistline is raised above the wearer's natural waist-line is called an empire waist. It can sometime be as high as right under the bust. Best worn on small-breasted, petite woman, the empire dress can also create the illusion of length to camouflage a bottom-heavy figure. Pronounced om-peer, the Empire dress was also called a sacque dress. It was fitted at the shoulders and full at the hips. These features, along with the gathering beneath the bosom, produced a de-emphasized waist and many pregnancies were hidden for months. The 1960s version was the tent or "baby doll dress" many times worn in transparent chiffon over a contrasting sewn-in slip.

Culottes

Culottes had the freedom of trousers, but the look of a full skirt. You could wear them to school because they looked like a skirt, and they were also great as sportswear. Nineteen sixty-five saw the premiere of these dresses in vibrant colored patterns and op-art styles which were especially popular as evening or party wear.

Sisters Genny, Josie, and Dorothy, 1964

Shirtwaist Dress

Shirtwaist dresses, based on the design of a man's shirt, had been worn as early as the first decade of the twentieth century. Simple and practical, they were not new in the 1950's, but they experienced a new burst of popularity at that time. Mademoiselle magazine wrote, "the wartime shirtwaister... flourished in the form of 1950's dresses which became almost symbolic of the housewife..." This utility look focused on the silhouette of square shoulders and short straight skirt, and often appeared in ads in *Good Housekeeping*, *Seventeen*, and *Mademoiselle*.

The inside cover of *Girls* and *Teens Merchandiser* viewed a more modern version of the shirtwaist with partly pushed-up cuff sleeves and shoe-string ties at the neck sewn in a sophisticated black-stripe cotton. Christian Dior's influence on the 1950's-style shirtwaist began with his "New Look" collection, which almost single-handedly defined the post-war silhouette. Although other designers were working with similar skirt shapes at the time, the fashion media credited Dior with the inception of the look.

Vogue reported that "the new shirtwaist" was the thing to wear if you were a young millionaire or a budget-conscious woman who shopped at J. C. Penney rather than Bergdorf Goodman.

Dior's version focused on a "nipped in" waist with full skirt. He often created the look of the tiny waist through boning within the bodice of the garment that reshaped the body. Often described as "pinched," the waistline of these dresses was probably the most difficult to achieve of the "New Look" elements. Shirtwaists were wonderful for women with small waists and large hips.

The shirtwaist was extremely versatile, and the style lent itself to sportswear, dinner dresses, evening ensembles, party dresses or housecoats. The shirtwaist could be given fullness via pleating, petticoats, flounces or crinolines. Pleating extra yardage became more popular as wartime fabric rationing was discontinued.

The "New Look" style was heavily marketed to the young woman because she was more interested in new

trends and more likely to adapt to change easily than her mother. The new shirtwaist dress became a staple in the American wardrobe because it was cheaply available in chain stores. Minor changes kept this dress consistently popular. The most significant change was in the use of patterned fabrics and floral prints.

The Shirtwaisted Woman

In the mid to late 1950's, television began to reinforce the shirtwaist as a mother's uniform on family comedy shows like *The Adventures of Ozzie and Harriet, Leave It to Beaver, Father Knows Best, Make Room for Daddy* and

Remember When We Wore——?

Blouses and Shirts

Angel Blouses
Nothing Blouses
Cha-Cha Blouses
Peasant Blouses
Nehru jackets
Mohair sweaters
Dickies under shirts

Dresses

Dresses or skirts at school [no
slacks for girls]
Tent dresses
Empire
Sack

Pants, Culottes/ Skirts

Peddle pushers
Hot pants
Kilt skirts with knee socks
Pleated skirts
Bermuda shorts with knee socks
Skirts that had to touch floor
when kneeling

Accessories

Fishnet stockings
Seamed nylons
Cats eye glasses
Scotch tape on bangs
and spit curls

Aqua Net hairspray
Pale frosted white lipstick

Cologne

Canoe
English Leather
Pub
Ambush
Jade East
British Sterling
Hai Karate
Brut
Evening in Paris
Blue Walz
Tabu

The Donna Reed Show. Women were shown doing housework in the most perfect of ensembles, including Dior-inspired shirtwaists, and wearing high heels and pearls.

Co-workers on *The Donna Reed Show* described her as "wife, mother, companion, booster, nurse, housekeeper, cook, laundress, gardener, bookkeeper, clubwoman, choir singer, PTA officer, Scout leader and at the same time, effervescent, immaculate and pretty." Her character was unrealistic but the ideals helped to solidify the shirtwaist dress as an icon of feminine perfection.

Women in high school and college received part of their fashion information from reading textbooks in their home economics class. One such book, *Clothing for Moderns,* listed the shirtwaist as fourth on the list of the seven basic garments every woman needed. It stated that the "casual shirtwaist or coat dress is for school, work, dates and travel."

Perhaps the more astounding revelation was that by 1967 the shirtwaist dress had become a cultural icon depicting the 1950's. Whenever a play, movie or

TV series featured the ideal woman, the costume designer had to at least consider the "New Look" shirtwaist. Films like *Pleasantville* and *Far From Heaven* showed housewives from the 1950's wearing the shirtwaist dress.

Padded Bras

Tiny waists and high, well-defined bosoms were emphasized in the 1950's and 60's. Whatever a woman's physical proportions, she tried to make her curves look well-edited in sheath dresses, pencil-slim skirts, and cinch belts. Some women required far more from a brassiere than stitches and straps. Of course, ingenious methods of faking an ample bosom have been used throughout history. But, the 1950's offered high-tech ploys. Foam rubber became the augmenter of choice. Eiderdown and felt were also used for "falsies." Some had removable pads inserted into special pockets but many were built right into the cups.

Names like True Form, Secret Charm, Radiant Security, Curves 2-U and Complement coaxed buyers to purchase these enhancers. The Tres Secrete developed by La Resista Company made an inflatable brassiere with a little plastic straw to blow up the desired cup size. Padding was not the only thing added to brassieres: Kabo offered the Bou-K-Bra which contained a removable "Scent Petal" secret pocket where personal cologne or perfume could be added for a touch of fragrance. Gem-Dandy offered the Mon-e-Bra with zippered front section between the cups to hold money or jewelry.

Nylons

In modern times fashion and skirt length have always influenced hosiery design. At the beginning of the twentieth century it was fashionable to wear skirts with long silk stockings. Later, machine-made, cotton knit stockings came into fashion with seams often ornamented by elaborate silk patterns or "clocks." With the arrival of synthetic fibers, hosiery or hose came to be popularly known as "nylons." Nylon stockings completely replaced the silk stocking which had seams up the back. A pair of nylons was sold in a thin box and wrapped in tissue paper. There were even stores that sold nothing but hosiery.

By the early Sixties, stockings were rapidly replaced by modern versions of the reinforced seamless heel and toe. They were made on circular knitting machines and shaped by tightening the stitches. Later, when skirts were very short, many women began to wear nylon tights instead of stockings. To show "a bit of stocking" was no longer accepted and nylons became nearly extinct as pantyhose gained in popularity. Fish net stockings were extremely popular in the mid 1960's.

Girdles

The girdle is defined as a "flexible, light-weight shaped corset made partly or entirely of elastic." Worn to confine the figure, especially through the hip line, girdles evolved continuously to take advantage of new fibers and fabric in response to each new silhouette in women's outerwear. Panty girdles came on the scene when substantial numbers of women began to wear pants. Initially, the girdles appealed to the younger woman, but eventually women of all ages wore some type of girdle.

In the famously unconstrained 1920's, teens and young women (who were collectively termed flappers) set aside the abhorred heavy corsets on which their mothers depended. Fashionable women often rolled the top of their stockings and limited their underwear to step-in panties or a wispy bandeau. As a contoured silhouette gradually began to return to women's fashions, however, flappers and other women accepted wearing garter belts and light girdles. Technology and fashion converged to produce girdles which sold by the millions, despite persistence of an economic depression. Unit sales of girdles topped 20.6 million in 1935 alone.

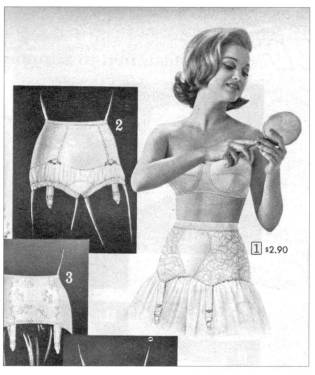

1 $2.90

Most panties had garters because stockings continued to be worn under pants, but a few styles featured removable garters or special leg bands that held down the girdle when socks were worn or when a woman went barelegged. Regular girdles were marketed for all purposes from housework to evening parties at prices ranging from 59 cents to 15 dollars. A girdle could be as short as eight inches, like a glorified garter belt, but most came in ten, twelve, fourteen and sixteen-inch lengths. They varied with the height of the wearer and her need for hip and waist control. Better known companies such as Maidenform, Formfit, Carter, Kayser and Munsingwear profited greatly as many women continued to wear girdles into the 1970's, whether they needed them or not.

for any type of hair
new
push button
Lilt
FOAM home permanent

Chapter 4

HAIR

Introduction

No woman can think back on the hairstyles of the fifties and sixties without being reminded of home permanents. I endured a lot of Toni and Lilt permanents in my childhood. My sister would roll those pink, plastic curling rods just short of yanking my hair out of my scalp and then drench each lock with that horrible-smelling curling solution. I had to wait for what seemed like an eternity for it to take affect, all the while enduring an itchy scalp and that caustic odor! For weeks afterward, as the odor lingered, everyone knew I had gotten a perm, if the tight curls hadn't tipped them off in the first place! But the result, wonderful frizzie curls that stuck out every which way on my head, was worth all the agony.

My first year in junior high school was a disaster for me. In the first place, I had lots of trouble simply getting ready in time to catch the bus. My first class was swimming and we wore those tight-fitting bathing caps that nearly cut off the circulation to the brain. When I took the cap off, my thick curly hair, which had been further keyed-up by the necessary home permanent, would spring back in every direction. Attempting to dry it with a wall-mounted hair-dryer only added to the general sense of confusion and disarray! Afterward, I'd have to try to make it to my second hour class, which was on the other side of the building. Needless to say, I was never on time and always looked a fright when I walked into Mrs. Bashara's English class.

My Hair

My hair has always been a source of worry, but also the part of me of which I am the most proud. Some say it's a blessing that I was born with lots of thick hair; but beleive me, it was also a problem figuring out what to do with so much of it.

As a child I spent many Saturday nights with my hair tied in white rags. My mother tore sheets in strips and wrapped my hair around them to make locks. They were pulled so tightly that it hurt my head. The sausage-like, coiled curlers were almost impossible to sleep on, which may explain why I was so crabby in church every Sunday morning. But, oh how beautiful those curls were! We don't have any photos of me in my red headed locks, and I was the only one to have red hair like my mother. I imagined she spent many nights with her hair wrapped in rags too when she was a girl. My grandmother used to create locks in my older sisters' hair using lard. She would smooth it on, then roll and tie the locks of hair with strips of cloth. I remember my sisters using pieces of tin foil to wrap their hair around for pin curls in the early 1950s.

From sheet strips, I graduated to spoolies. Spoolies were pink rubber gadgets which resembled mushrooms, with holes through them. I would wrap my hair around the shaft of the spoolie, then snap the cap of the mushroom part down over my curled hair. When I took them out, they made a popping sound. They came in pastel colors, but were also hard to sleep in.

As I got a little older, my hair was set in sponge rollers, which were always pink. You can still buy them today, made by Goody Hair Supplies, which is a very old company. One of my older sister's jobs was to set my hair on Saturday nights, the day before going to Mass. When Dorothy did it, she pulled my hair so hard my head always ached in the morning. I think she was acting out some sort of sibling rivalry. I often tried to corner one of my two other older ones, Josie or Phyllis, instead, but they were usually busy on Saturday nights and I had to beg them to do it. Sometimes I even made bargains with them. I could usually count on Josie. She would say, "Come on, I'll set your hair in pin curls." When she got married and moved away, it was a blow to us all as she was always so caring .

Eventually I learned to set my own hair and started using brush rollers. Some were made of hard plastic and others had stiff bristles on the inside, which were covered with stretchy netting-like material. In the sixties, I used hair rollers the size of soup cans. We also used gobs of hair gel called Dippity Do that I must have used by the crate.

Most girls had their own personal hairdryers with hoses and plastic caps in those days. I sat under a hooded hair dryer, sometimes for nearly an hour, depending on the length of my hair. After drying the hair I would tease or backcomb it to give it maximum height. This conglomeration was held together by lots of aerosol hairspray. (Aqua Net was the only one we could afford.) Sometimes the process took two hours!

The main ingredients of hairspray were alcohol and lacquer. By the mid sixties, hairspray was the number one beauty aid. Hairdressers talked about how sticky the floor would become by the end of the day, and the lacquer would also be all over their skin and clothes. Some of the most beautiful hairstyles came from this period and were works of art. To preserve the styles until the next day, women would wrap toilet paper around their heads before they went to bed at night. This trend will forever be looked back upon with an amused shake of the head. It was the era of Big Hair.

The lacquer insured that your hair would hold its shape, even in a tornado. The tighter the rat, the puffier the hair stayed. A good backcomb job was almost impossible to get out without first washing your hair. My boyfriend, now my husband, used to pace the floor in impatience while he waited for me as I did my hair. I think it was worth the wait. His family made fun of the time I was in the bathroom, teasing, "Is she still in there?" But, they didn't understand I had a lot of hair and wanted it to look just so.

The sixties was also a time to have smooth hair, so in reality I was going through double trouble to straighten my hair. I went

through a phase of ironing my hair, but that didn't last long. Some of the popular hairstyles were the Sassoon, Flip, China Doll and Grecian Curls. We spent a great deal of time and money on our very sculptured hair back then. Also, there was the style of having your hair cut longer on one side. The pixie, with the hair cut really short, was the craze in the early sixties. The Bun and the French roll were also popular, and the pony and pigtails never went out of style.

It's fun to look back at old pictures and laugh at the hairdos and crazy clothes we used to wear. I find it amazing that I wear my hair short today, and in as simple a style as I can get. I spend only about ten to fifteen minutes on it daily and sometimes not even that. I suppose the blessing is that now that I am older, and many of my friends and family members are losing their hair, mine remains thick.

Hair Dye

When I was fifteen, I dyed my hair dark brown and it came out purple. I freaked. I couldn't leave the house or let my mother see because she didn't know I had dyed my hair in the first place. My best friend Pat went to the drugstore and got a bottle of Hilex bleach and hydrogen peroxide, which turned my hair stark white. The only thing I could do then was cover it with a wig, but the first time I took the wig off there were little clumps of hair missing on my head which took a long time to grow out again. I had to keep dying it a deep red, which was the only color that would cover bleached white.

How to Create a French Roll

This style had various names, though French Roll and French Pleat were the most common. Here are the steps you need to create this famous hairstyle.

1. Brush all tangles from hair.
2. Pull all the hair from one side of your head to the back and hold in place by crisscrossing the bobby pins

vertically up the back of the head. This should keep your style smooth.

3. Bring the hair from the other side to the back of the head and begin forming the roll. It is very important to keep the roll as smooth as possible. When this step has been completed, pin it in place, covering the crisscrossed bobby pins from the last step.

4. New pins should be slid into the edge of the roll and completely hidden from view.

5. Mist with your favorite styling spray

Beehive

Fashionable hairstyles began the decade with a simple ponytail and ended with a complex beehive arrangement. Popular hairstyles in the 1950s and 60s were the poodle cut and French Roll. The later years of the 60s had the beehive. Around 1964, high school girls took the bouffant to new heights. (The bouffant was also called a "beehive".) Dusty Springfield, a famous singer of the times, had a beehive and eye make-up that were copied throughout Britain. Lavish backcombing was sprayed, then teased into a high mound.

Hairpieces made the beehive bigger. Cascades and falls were added to make quick hairstyles. Synthetic hair was called Dynel. A woman could go to a wig or department store and the technician would blend the Dynel to match her own hair color. It was then braided, wound around a stuffing pad, then pinned on top of her head. Dynel was a big fashion statement in 1966.

A famous Urban Legend that surfaced during this time was of a high school girl who had the biggest hairstyle in school. As she sat in class, she used her pencil point to itch inside her hairdo. Unknown, and lurking inside this massive hairstyle was a black widow's nest. The teen poked the spider with her pencil, it bit her and she died from the bite right there in history class. Top that one for freaky incidents!

After the beehive came the Beatle cut and then Vidal Sassoon's five-point-cut, which was a bobbed style. Mary Quant, a leading fashion force in the 1960s famed for her pop art designs, miniskirt, and hot pants, sported a Sassoon haircut of a soft fringed cut.

The Breck Girl

In 1936, Edward Breck hired Charles Sheldon to draw women for his shampoo advertisements. Sheldon's early portraits were done in pastels with a focus on soft haloes of light. He created romantic images of feminine beauty and purity, preferring to draw "real women."

In the late 1950s, Ralph William Williams became the new Breck artist. Unlike Sheldon, he often used professional women. Some of the famous "Breck Girls" were Kim Basinger, Brooke Shields, Erin Gray, Cheryl Tiegs, Jaclyn Smith and Cybil Sheperd.

Breck ads ran regularly in magazines like *Ladies Home Journal, Woman's Home Companion, Seventeen, Vogue, Glamour* and *Harpers Bazaar.* These ads were most often featured on the back cover. After Williams' death in 1976, the advertising tradition stopped. Breck Girl ads are now in the Smithsonian's National Museum of American History.

The First Home Permanents

When the Toni Home Permanent was introduced, it opened the door for women who wanted a permanent wave without going to the beauty parlor and paying a high price for one. The Toni Company continued to make their product better though they faced stiff competiton from other brands as well as professional hairdressers.

Bill Cullen began advertising the Toni Home Permanent on the radio's serial program, This is Nora Drake, and the popular drama, Casey—Crime Photographer. The ad featured identical twin sisters who had identical-looking waves. There was only one difference. One had her hair done at a beauty parlor while the other used Toni. The classic question Cullen asked his listeners was,

"Which twin has the Toni?" Unless people were told they couldn't tell. (The magazine ads gave the answer in small print.)

The cost of a professional wave was $15 and the Toni Kit sold for $2. It was easy to use a home permanent and the other $13 could be spent on necessities. After the kit was purchased, the Toni refill that included a bottle of waving lotion was available for $1.

The Toni Home Permanent became an instant success, but before long other similar products had entered the market. The promotion of the Toni Twins was so popular that the phrase; "Which Twin has the Toni?" became part of the everyday language of the time. Also, the name Toni became synonymous with the words 'home permanent.'

Later, the company introduced Toni Crème Shampoo, which was also advertised by Bill Cullen. He claimed that it gave its users soft water shampooing even in water hard as concrete. This ad also featured the Toni Twins. The Toni Company later focused on products like White Rain, Spin Curlers, Silver Curl, Tame, Pamper, Adorn, Viv, and Deep Magic. The Gillette Safety Razor Company acquired the Toni Company in 1948 and sold hair and skin products for women and shaving products for men.

According to a *Life* magazine feature story, "every woman in the 1950s got at least one home perm." Home permanent ads were big business in the fifties. Makers of Prom home permanents sponsored a number of radio shows. The Lilt Company took their advertising to the top and hired Lucille Ball, star of the popular sitcom *I Love Lucy*.

In a 1950 ad for Rayve, Mary Martin, star of the Broadway musical, *South Pacific*, advertised twelve new Mary Martin curlers plus a Rayve refill for only $1.29. Because some customers felt that home perms gave overly curly results, Bobbi Home Permanent pictured softer, wavier hair in more casual styles. Shadow Wave was a perm made by the Pepsodent Company.

The Richard Hudnut Home Permanent for children advertised in one issue of Parents Magazine that it was safe and was the only permanent specifically designed for hard-to-wave children's hair. Tonette was also a popular perm for children.

Until recently a number of brands of home permanent kits were still available, but their numbers have decreased. Permanent waves are simply not as popular as they were in the 1980s.

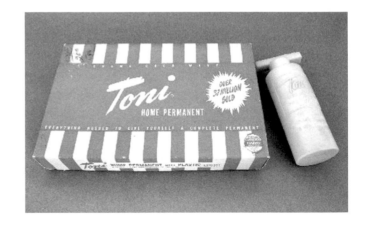

– Hairdos from 1967 –

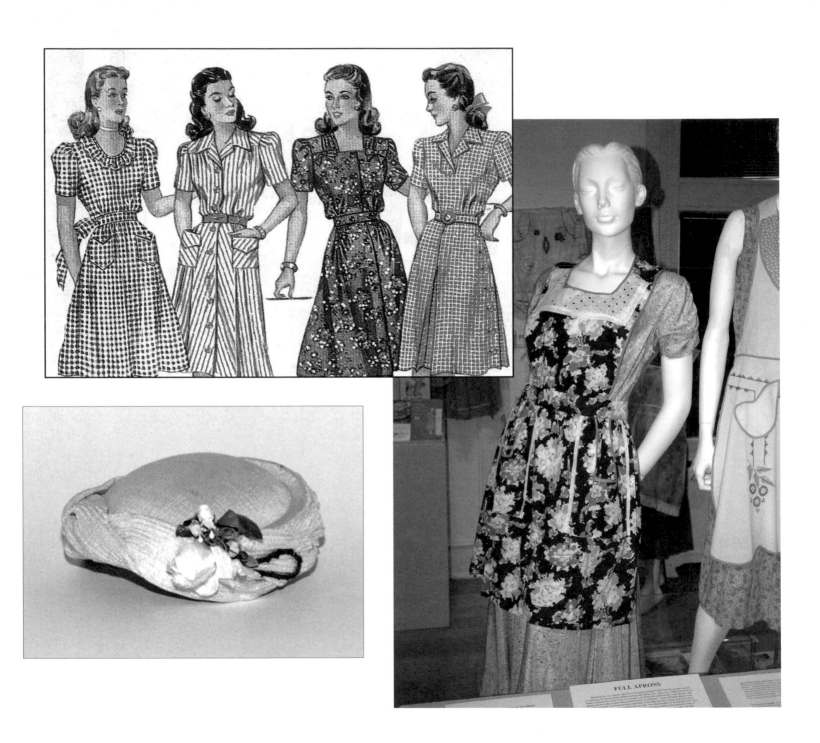

FULL APRONS

Chapter 5

WHAT OUR PARENTS WORE:
Hats, Aprons, and Housedresses

Introduction

I saw a picture once of an older lady wearing a house dress. She had a kerchief on her head, and on her feet she wore black chunky-heel shoes that tied in the front with little holes in them—the kind that old maids and schoolteachers wore. I loved seeing that picture because it reminded me of the older ladies who lived in my neighborhood when I was growing up. It reminded me of simpler times when ladies were valued for who they were, their caring natures and smiles, and not the way they looked. I miss those times. Whenever I see old hats, aprons and housedresses it takes me back in time.

Housedresses

There was a time when most women wore housedresses. They were made of cotton prints in muted rainbow colors. They were made to be worn in the house for cleaning and doing other household chores but my mother wore hers all the time. She never wore pants.

Many women sewed their own housedresses but my mother's were store bought. There was a little dry goods store within walking distance of our house that sold old-fashioned items like aprons, housedresses and colorful kerchiefs. I didn't like that store because it was too old-world for me, but now I wish I could go back there. To me this store was the epitome of personal service and it was the gateway to a trip back in time.

Many women would change their housedress with great ease if someone came to call, switching in a hurry to a day dress for unannounced visitors like the Fuller Brush man or the priest. My mother, a farm woman who had moved to the city, would simply slip off her apron before she opened the door for any guest who arrived. Farm women wore housedresses to town but it was not considered proper etiquette for city women to do so.

Women from the farm had a ready source of fabric for making housedresses. Feed sacks came in cotton prints and provided about a yard of usable fabric. Two or three bags of a matching pattern that could be used to sew a dress was the best purchase a farmer could make.

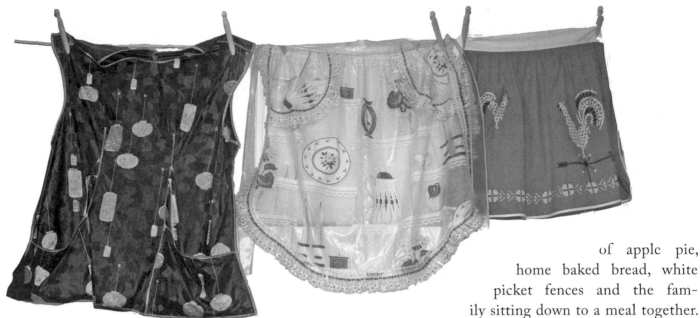

Aprons

Aprons were an important part of family life and really became popular during the 1940s. Every housewife had a wide assortment of them. Some were store-bought and others were lovingly sewn or hand embroidered. For years the first project in Home Economics class or 4 H Club was to make an apron. Of course, this could be personalized in whatever way the young lady chose. It was the beginning of her self expression.

Aprons worn by our mothers, aunts, grandmothers and great-aunts were seen on holidays and special occasions, but also while involved in the every day tasks of baking and cooking. When we see them today, they evoke memories of the kitchen in simpler times—

of apple pie, home baked bread, white picket fences and the family sitting down to a meal together.

Aprons were a protection from the spatters and drips that occurred in a busy kitchen, but more than that, they were an expression of the creativity of the women who made and wore them. They told the story of women's lives and roles. They were a symbol of love, security, and stability.

My mother's aprons hung neatly behind the door in the pantry. She had seven of them—one for every day of the week. She had a red checked apron and a blue polka dot apron, but the ones I loved and remembered the most were flowered; the kind that were covered with prints and flowers and edged with piping and rickrack. Most of them were lavender, my mother's favorite color.

Full Aprons

Spanning the last century, the full apron or bib apron perhaps brings back the greatest number of memories for those whose mothers and grandmothers were rarely seen without one. Made to protect the entire front of a woman's clothing from cooking spills and splashes, full aprons are best seen as three-dimensional pieces of sculpture. These utilitarian aprons were cut and contoured to fit the many possible shapes and sizes of a female body. The full apron needed to fit securely over the shoulders or

around the neck while at the same time fit comfortably around the waist and hang loosely at the bottom for ease of movement. The backs of full aprons often provide an interesting array of creative designs such as crossed straps or special trim.

Sometimes called a "utility" or "farm apron," in many ways these were the workhorses of women's aprons. They were generally not made to impress the neighbors or show off at a church social, but to endure the grind of daily housework. Unlike the half apron, the full apron was the least likely to be elaborately decorated and the most likely to get worn out and thrown away. Midsections often had the printed design worn off from continual movement against the lip of a sink or the edge of a washtub. The fabric might grow thin and worn from the wearer repeatedly holding a bowl to her waist while stirring a cake or starting a batch of bread dough. Wearers would repeatedly wipe their hands on the lower corners of the apron after cutting meat or polishing furniture, which resulted in multi-colored stains. The utility apron ties would fray and tear after years of being tied and untied every time a woman went to and from her domestic chores. But those that survived whole and complete testify to the art and beauty of a well-made apron.

Hostess Aprons

Patterns galore were available during the 1950s and 1960s for the "hostess" apron, an apron worn by the "woman of the house" as she served dinner and dessert to the family's guests. Meant to impress rather than get dirty, these aprons were most often made from lightweight or sheer fabrics such as organdy and batiste. Coming in a wide range of colors, including the 1950s colors of popular pink and black, these fabrics were designed to go with each and every party dress in a woman's closet.

The most common design of the hostess apron used organdy for the main body of the apron with plain or print cotton added on as trim, patterns or pockets. Rickrack, bias tape and other decorations were also added. These aprons were obviously not only to match the hostess' dress but also to demonstrate her creativity and sewing skills.

Another common use of the hostess apron was as a gift at weddings and showers. Mothers and/or daughters would make matching hostess aprons for the women serving the wedding meal in the church basement or at the shower, and then give them the aprons as mementos and tokens of appreciation.

Kitsch and Novelty Aprons

One of the popular Kitsch apron patterns of the late 1960s was the "bloomer" or pants apron. At a time when women were primarily wearing dresses and skirts, this odd-looking apron may well have served as a means to try out "wearing the pants" in the family.

Novelty aprons began to appear in the 1950s and continue on in today's market. Aprons with printed messages such as "How to Keep Your Husband," or "I may be an Oldie but I'm a Goodie" and "Kiss the Cook" might even be appreciated as the forerunners to the message ladened T-shirts of today.

Gingham Aprons

Much has been written about the gingham apron whose popularity spanned most of the twentieth

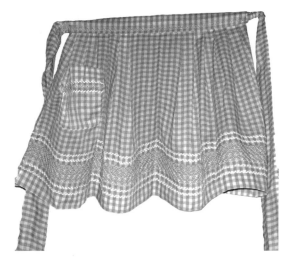

making the apron design appear to have a third element of color. Smocking, "pulled thread" work, rick-rack, lace, metallic threads, waist pleats and pockets were among the many complimentary essentials used to give each gingham apron its unassuming yet delightful personality.

Crocheted Apron

century. Appearing in stores as early as the 1920s, "gingham" referred to all fabrics with a checkered weave. The most common gingham cloth was a yarn-dyed cotton of white and colored threads forming the uniform patterns of a checkerboard design. Each checkered square might measure anywhere from a full inch to 1/16 of an inch in width.

Whatever the width of the gingham design might happen to be, women created a vast array of decorative aprons from the cloth. With colors running the gamut from primary colors to pastels with white check, the gingham apron became an able testament to women's innovation and creative energies.

The most common gingham apron was a half apron decorated with cotton embroidery floss. Cross stitch, embroidery stitches such as the "chicken scratch, fly stitch, stairstep and feather stitch" as well as the "Tenerife lace stitch" were used to create colorful border designs. Darker hues of the same-checkered color might be stitched unto the white squares

Crocheted aprons were very popular in the 1940s. Sewed with handmade cotton threads, these aprons came in a wide variety of patterns and colors. Perhaps the two most common designs were the "chevron" and the elaborate "pineapple" pattern with its flaring and flamboyant bottom.

White and cream were often-used as colors for the hand-crocheted aprons, while accents of variegated thread created delicate and beautiful designs within designs. Most often the crocheted apron was a half apron, but occasionally the maker would add a small upper panel to pin onto a dress top.

Women would add their signature touch to these aprons by crocheting on a matching pocket or trimming the waistband and ties with special crocheted stitches. As most crocheted aprons appeared to have never been used, it is possible that their function was mostly as gifts to look at and admire among women relatives and friends.

Hats

There was once a tradition that blended high fashion, deep spirituality, and respect for your ancestors—the tradition of women wearing elaborate hats to church. Fur hats, velvet hats, fabric hats, and hats with artful concoctions of feathers were proudly displayed. Some thought the more stuff you could fit on your hat the better. Hats were fussed over, treasured, even coveted by women of all ages. Hats concealed but mostly revealed a great deal about those who wore them and their world. In scores of American churches every Sunday, faith and fashion united. From the demure to the "why'd you have to sit down in front of me" variety, hats were always more than what they seemed. It was not just about self-glorification, but also about glorifying God.

The tradition of hats honoring spiritual beliefs still exists in African-American churches. Many women don't just wear a hat to church; they continue the tradition of making a statement with their hat. Hats were an expression of belief in oneself even when the messages from society were quite different. Slave women covered their heads with bandanas and decorated them with wildflowers.

If a woman wanted to show off her hat and be in style—she would wear it in church. A hat might serve as an instant symbol that a woman had arrived and was on her feet. In time hats became more and more flamboyant as trinkets and adornments were added, the intended meaning being, "Look how God has blessed me."

Young children were told, "God said, cover your head—doesn't have to be a hat—just cover your head when you come into the house of the Lord." Some women back then thought that a person was not properly dressed unless she had a hat on. "Hat-attitude" is the way a hat makes you feel when you walked into church. Sometimes hats were made from the same material as the accompanying dress. Some were plain, but showed off the wearer's sewing ability and creativity. Many were proud to wear what their Mamas had made.

Hats with plumes have historically been a status symbol and a sign of economic position. At the turn of the century, both men and women changed their hats depending upon their activity. An attitude was revealed by when, where and how they wore their hats and was expressed in the tilt of the hat swaying to music. There were Mother's Day Hats, church-going hats, funeral hats and even hats worn in the tobacco fields.

Audrey Hepburn made the wide-brimmed picture hat popular in the movie *Breakfast at Tiffany's*. It was black straw trimmed with a white ribbon band. Of all the fashion trends set by First Lady Jackie Kennedy, she will be remembered most for her trademark hat. It was called a "pillbox" because it looked as if it was designed to hold pills. While Mrs. Kennedy is credited with bringing the hat to the masses, the pill box hat has existed in different forms since the 1930s. In fact, Mrs. Kennedy was not even the first First Lady to wear one, as the First Lady of Mexico preceded her by a year or so.

Other hat styles include the beret, cloche, turban, halo, and bouffant flower cloche. Then we have the half-hat which allows a woman to place a hat on top of her head in a way that won't mess up her hairdo. The feather clip, velvet clip with bows or flowers, braided circlet with tiny butterfly bows on misty veiling, and the velvet ringlet with flirtatious chenille-dotted veil were popular for almost any occasion.

In earlier times men's hat-making shops were called haberdashers, and women's were called milliners. The wearing of hats to church and for dressing up became less popular in the late 1960s, in part as a result of Vatican II, when the rules of the Catholic Church became more relaxed and women were no longer required to cover their heads.

Hankies

We live in a society that no longer uses hankies, preferring disposable, inelegant paper. But there was a time when beautiful cloth handkerchiefs were widely used, and they were often a thing of beauty. Beautiful cloth handkerchiefs were often given as gifts. They were stored carefully and treasured by their owners. Many of them had unusual shapes, themes, designer labels, elaborate needlework, fabric printing, embroidery, lace and other edging.

Women used hankies not only for hygienic reasons, but also for other personal reasons such as waving at men. It was not just in the movies that ladies dropped their hankies in calculated fashion to be retrieved by a passing man, who would return it and thus initiate an introduction. The use of the word "handkerchief" has been traced to a dictionary entry from 1530, and the custom of carrying a small piece of cloth for wiping a nose or dabbing a tear surely started long before that date.

In the early twentieth century, no lady or gentleman would be considered properly dressed who did not carry a handkerchief, typically monogrammed with a single initial, representing her first name or his last name. Some of the more unusual handkerchiefs in the early twentieth century were the black-edged "mourning hankies," first made popular by Queen Victoria when her husband, Prince Albert, died in 1871. Children's hankie toys, such as a teddy bear or miniature briefcase, came with a hankie attached.

World War I brought the tradition of the "sweetheart gift," where an item could be purchased by a serviceman overseas to ship home to the girlfriend, sister or mom left behind. Handkerchiefs decorated with patriotic themes and elegantly posed soldiers rendered in ink printing and hand coloring were part of this custom, which continued in World War II. Men who served in that war recalled "sweetheart" handkerchiefs for sale at the PX for mailing home.

In between the wars and on the home front, handkerchiefs were miniature models for the styles of the times. Art deco motifs appeared in the 1920s, primarily on packaging, while handkerchiefs themselves often had more conservative bits of embroidery. In the 1930s and 1940s came a flowering of printed fabrics from bold geometrics to realistic birds and vegetation. Hankies also served as souvenirs, commemorating events such as expositions, fairs, and family vacations.

During the 1940s and 1950s there was a burst of creativity in many of the arts, including fabric design, and this was a good era for hankies. Round hankies even made a brief appearance in the late 40s and early 50s. Children's hankies were designed by artists like Tom Lamb, an illustrator for Walt Disney, decorated with cartoon characters.

In the 1950s, people found new uses and novel ways

The hanky department at Woolworth's 1956

to display hankies. They were incorporated into hand-made aprons and deployed in "hanky umbrella" party favors. Children gave teachers handkerchiefs for birthdays and Christmas gifts. Many fine hankies were sewn into pillows and quilts, and the fancy handkerchiefs that were used in wedding ceremonies were later used to make bonnets for the soon-to-arrive babies. The primary fabrics used to make hankies were cotton, silk, linen and nylon. Until not too long ago, you could still buy novelty hankies edged in lace or machine embroidered at old-fashioned drug and variety stores.

But that golden age of hankies is now just a memory. Very few Americans use hankies any more. As with many things of the past, part of the blame must fall upon the development of new technologies and products. The cartoon schoolgirl Little Lulu was the spokesperson for Kleenex in the 1940s and 1950s, and even starred in a

Little Golden Book that incorporated Kleenex tissues into its design. In a series of magazine ads she advocated using Kleenex not only to catch sneezes, but as coasters and to wipe up small spills. Matters of cost aside, the rising popularity of disposable facial tissue was driven by fears of contamination. Americans began to use Kleenex instead of hankies because they were more hygienic. Once you'd used one, you could just throw it away.

Chapter 6

DRIVE-INS:

The Place to Be on a Saturday Night

Drive-In Movies

One of the most beloved symbols of the fifties was the drive-in movie theater. Many teenagers frequented the drive-in on a weekly basis. There have always been a number of activities tied to drive-in theaters that have nothing to do with films. The drive-in has always been used as a gathering place for friends, a locale providing an excuse for enjoying the outdoors at night and, most notably, a popular venue for young couples to... not watch movies.

During the 50's drive-ins were at their peak of popularity. And with all that was happening there on any given night, a teenager of that era might have even commented, 'They show movies there?"

In order to generate greater interest (and revenue), drive-in owners would often offer carload prices, "spectacular" prizes, and anything else they could think of to increase profitability. But nothing compared to the profit potential of a drive-in feature that became many people's favorite part of the outdoor movie-going experience—snacks.

The snack bar has always provided theater owners with their largest profit margin. Drive-ins managed to exploit this vein even more effectively by offering a more varied menu than their indoor counterparts. And even

though many patrons continue to bring their own food to drive-ins to this day, few can resist the allure of drive-in hot dogs, hamburgers, and some of the tastiest and least healthy cuisine ever consumed by humans.

Though drive-ins were notoriously convenient hang-outs for adolescents, they were also a boon to families with young children. Mom and dad could enjoy watching a film on the big screen at a reasonable price, while the kids dozed in the back seat in their feetie pajamas with pillows, stuffed animals and blankets. It was common for families to bring sleeping bags for their children who often nodded off before the last feature even started. Station wagons were the perfect vehicle for such excursions. The only problem was that sometimes the parents fell asleep too.

Many of us who can barely remember what films we saw at the drive-in, nevertheless have a vivid memory of singing and dancing hot dogs, soda pop, popcorn and chocolate bars, enticing us to visit the concession stand. How many remember having trouble finding your way back to your car after a trip to the concession stand? Some people called the drive-ins "passion pits" and parents complained that children who lived nearby could see risque movies from their bedroom windows.

Yet many of the movies targeted a teen or adult audience. Examples were the beach movies of the 60's and the movies in the 70's like "The Van" "Texas Cheerleaders" and other Sci-fi and horror pictures. All the better for teenage snuggling.

Theater owners often complained about customers who drove away after a show with the speakers still attached to the partially-rolled-down window of their car. But this was seldom intentional, and the damage to the vehicle might well be more severe than the mere loss of a transmission cable. (At a certain point drive-ins began to deliver the audio feed via radio waves.)

Many drive-in theaters opened their gates as much as three hours before the movies started, allowing families to bring the kids early—while also insuring that the theater would sell more high-priced food. Some drive-ins began to serve a wide variety of dinners such as fried chicken, barbecued sandwiches, hamburgers, and pizza. A few theater owners even gave their customers the convenience of ordering meals from their car, to be delivered later by a car hop.

One of the largest Drive-In Theaters was the All-Weather Drive-In located in Capiague, New York, which held parking spaces for 2,500 cars and also had a playground, a cafeteria, a restaurant with full dinners, and a 1,200-seat indoor viewing area that was heated and air-conditioned. A shuttle train took customers from their cars to the various areas on the 28 acre grounds.

Twin City Drive-In Theatres

In 1966 during their peak period, there were 19 drive-ins in the Twin Cities that drew carloads of families and teenagers on muggy summer nights. Cars crowded into the drive-ins and the children enjoyed the movies in comfort while sitting on the front of cars or in lawn chairs.

In those days the Colonial Drive-In located in Medina was one of the newest. Its grand opening was on July 1st, 1966. Among the Colonial's virtues, according to an advertisement of the time, were "the latest in playground equipment, delicious and quick service snack bar. New aluminum Glo screen for better viewing, finest speakers for better sound, Nature's Air-Conditioned Drive-In…High on a hill free of mosquitoes. Every windshield washed by attendants for better viewing."

As the times and the competition changed, the theaters made every effort to keep pace. They purchased new projectors that did a better job of throwing light more than 400 feet onto a screen 120 feet wide. Movie sound moved from the theater's own speakers to a post, then to a low-level radio transmission that patrons picked up on their car radios. That move also helped reduce vandalism problems with the speakers.

Why did the drive-ins fall from favor? Among the factors were: smaller families, smaller cars, Daylight Saving Time, Minnesota's long summer twilight, a band on DDT formerly used to combat mosquitoes, and the growth of videocassette machines.

By 1980 the number of outdoor theaters had dropped to 900 nation-wide. As cities and suburbs grew and land became more valuable, drive-in theaters were made into shopping centers and parking lots. But there are still a few in operation in outlying areas. The relaxed setting will always have its appeal, not to mention the nostalgia.

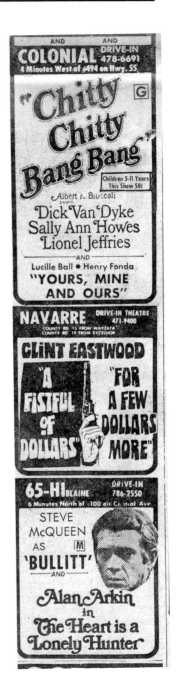

When the drive-in theaters closed, the drive-in subculture went with them. We can only look back fondly at such things as sneaking in extra viewers in car trunks; watching count-down clocks on the screen before the show started; backseat necking; horn-honking during steamy/exciting/cliffhanging scenes. Intermission filler and promos designed to drive you crazy, to the point where you would be out of the car and in line at the snack bar in no time.

At one point a garbled voice would break in on the car speaker, "Would Patrice Hehmer please come to the snack bar?" Honk! HonkHonhonkhonk!!! Hooooonnnnnkkk! This is the cue for everyone to start laying on the horn, for only one reason; everyone's a comedian at the drive-in.

Well, that about describes the history of drive-ins. There are still some being built, but many more are closing. The heyday is gone, and many theatres even pulled out their playground equipment in the 70's since few families were attending.

The Drive-Ins that have closed their gates for good have met diverse fates. The Hilltop is now a K Mart.

The Minnehaha, which closed in 1984, is now a part of 3M Company's park preserve. Navarre now holds a townhouse development. 7-Hi is now a K Mart and B. Dalton Bookstore. 100 Twin closed in 1986 and is now Lake Pointe Corporate Center. Colonial closed in 1984.

Starlite became a Target Store and Shopping Center. France Avenue was torn down in 1985 to make the Shelard/Ramada hotel and office complex.

At last count, only six drive-ins are still in operation in the Twin Cities area—the Flying Cloud, Maple Leaf, Vali-Hi, St.Croix Hilltop, 65 Hi and Cottage View.

Twin City Drive-in Movie Locations

Bloomington—E.78th Street at 12th Avenue S

Rose—Snelling Avenue at County Road C
    in Roseville

Starlite—Highways 52 and 152 in Brooklyn Park

Lucky Twin—Highway 13 E of 35W in Burnsville

65 Hi—101st Street and Central Avenue NE
    in Blaine

Navarre—County Road 15, between Spring Park
    and Minnetonka Beach

7 Hi—SE corner of Highways 7 and 101
    in Minnetonka

Mann France Avenue—W of France Avenue just
    north of 494 in Edina

Coon Rapids—Highway 10 & E. River Road

Hilltop—47th Street & Central Avenue NE

Flying Cloud—Highways 169 & 212
    in Eden Prairie

100 Twin—Highways 694 and Central Avenue
    in Fridley

Maple Leaf—Highways 36 and 61 in Maplewood

Colonial Drive-in—Highways 55 & 101 in Medina

Vali-Hi—11260 Hudson Blvd. in Lake Elmo

Cottage View—9338 S Point Douglas Road
    in Cottage Grove

St. Croix Hilltop—Across St. Croix River
    from Stillwater in Wisconsin

Minnehaha—Minnehaha Avenue and E McKnight
    Road St. Paul

Corral—S Robert Street and Mendota Rd
    in West St. Paul

Pretending to be the Singing Popcorn Box

Joannie Moses

Movies, I've always loved movies. I remember in the mid-50's going to Cinerama, the forerunner of I-Max, in downtown Minneapolis and people around me actually getting sick from the "rides" on the screen. I thought the downtown theaters were the most beautiful places in the world, even more lovely than our church or the St. Paul Athletic Club. Some of the flicks they were showing made them even more dear to me. The Little Edythe Busch Theater had live plays with real people!

Not all movies were spectacular, but I think I viewed more than my share of extravaganzas. One of my favorite movies was "A Star Is Born" in downtown St. Paul, but neighborhood theaters were a great value. We went to the neighborhood theater for every Bible-based show that came out in the fifties—*Ben-Hur, The Robe, The Bible, and The Ten Commandments.* It only cost twenty-five cents for magnificent matinees. Snacks were not expensive and the seats were worn and comfortable. Architectural surroundings were nice, too.

In those older, smaller theaters one could really relate to the actors and their plights. I still could cry for Anastasia or Bambi and the emotions they evoked.

But my all-time favorite way to see a movie was at the Rose Drive-In Theater at County Road C and Snelling. In 1952, Mother had a Buick "woody" convertible that was perfect for movie-going! She filled a big brown grocery bag with hot buttered popcorn and drove to A&W for quarts of root beer in frosty brown bottles with little paper cups. We always took my brother's friend Curt and sometimes other neighborhood kids. We threw lawn chairs in the trunk. Some of us sat outside the car, some inside and some on top (except with the "ragtop.") For the first fifteen minutes after we arrived, we were trapped in the car with the windows up while the entire lot was sprayed with mosquito poison. As soon as the fog cleared we romped to the concession stand or the swing set to check out who else was there. We didn't have city playgrounds out in the Roseville sticks, so this place was Heaven to us. After a few minutes of swing-set play, the boys spread out and used the parked cars as strategically placed Army tanks. They imagined they were shooting it out as they played war while waiting for the sun to set.

We girls played during the big countdown until showtime. Of course, we pretended that we were the singing popcorn box, candy, or drink cups on legs. No one wanted to be the wiener though! We had lots of silly fun until the cartoons—then we had serious fun.

Then, finally, we returned to our family car as the

feature film began. We were awed by the huge faces of Marlon Brando or Grace Kelly or whoever's face was on this giant screen towering over our little car—their nostrils were bigger than our heads. And the stars' voices would crackle in from a speaker attached to the driver's window. There was nothing better in the whole world!

Drive-In Theaters had their specialties. We loved the French fries at the Stillwater Theater and the onion rings were the best at the Maple Leaf. There was a swing set at the 100 Twin and the Rose. Some people would sneak in friends hidden in the trunk to avoid paying for each person, though many theaters charged by the carload. Dusk to Dawn meant all night movies—a car load of teens that were scared out of their wits because the shows were often horror movies.

At age fifteen, when I got my driver's license, I collected directions to most of the drive-ins in the greater metropolitan area. I recall one month when I carted my girlfriends to Gone with the Wind five separate times - to the Corral on South Robert, the Lucky Twin, the 100 Twin, the Maple leaf, and finally to the Bloomington Drive-In, where we sat through the whole four hours in pouring rain. We were in a Bonneville convertible that rocked and bounced against the stormy wind gusts, but we stayed in the car

because it was surrounded by deep puddles. It was great! The thunder and lightning even added to the drama. An experience like that could spoil anyone for today's megaplex theater-going.

A little environmental reflection...

I am surprised that I never heard of any movie companies being sued for exposure to that stinky mist of mosquito poison! Surely it must have caused serious diseases, birth defects or even brain damage! Lawyers have sued everything from barn-cleaning chemicals to food additives for being carcinogens, and ground water toxins to medications for causing malformations. Yet, has anyone ever questioned whether that foul-smelling, bitter-tasting air pollutant (was it DDT?) to which we were willingly and copiously exposed at drive-in theaters has caused my generation to become Goldwater Young Republicans or Flower Children. And all the side-effects that imply—communal sexual deviants, drug-craving addicts, bra-burners, and so on? Sounds like a valid study to me. If Agent Orange can do all the harm which we have seen in our Viet Nam vet friends, then how widespread could the effects of bug spray 1950's-style be?

Maybe during his formative years Charles Manson ran a bug-bomber at the local drive-in. It's worth checking into.

A Tank of My Own

Memories of the Lyndale Drive-In

Richard Worthing

In the summer of 1957, after my sophomore year, my dad bought a 1947 Pontiac from one of his customers for two hundred dollars, essentially so I could drive to school. I would be mobile. I could get home after practice without having to bum a ride. Plus, I would have prospects. The Pontiac's cavernous frame provided ample room for friends. It was ponderous, dark green, and nicknamed "Sherman" after the popular tank. Doug Shaw, a friend living on 43rd and Dupont, had shotgun on the way to school. Doug's younger brother, Bruce, and Bruce's friend Ralph Burnett sat in the back. We were just being nice letting kids that young tag along in my four-door tank, a stick on the column, and vast, flat seats across the width of the car. The car created great space with its high ceiling and expansive back seat, perfect for a small crowd intent on meeting someone at the drive-in.

Soon after getting the car, I bought a cut-off, a small device that attaches to the exhaust from the manifold. Then I had to convince Bobby Brandt and Johnny Mogan to help me put it on. If you throw the switch on the floor, you cut the flow of exhaust to the tail pipe just before it gets to the muffler: wham! You have an old Pontiac floating along on ancient shocks, sounding like a World War II tank. They heard us coming, although we had to be careful not to use it too often because I drove too fast and didn't want too much attention. After "we" installed the cut-off, the car was never really quiet again. There was always leakage and at least a low rumble to announce and reiterate our presence.

Some nights we cruised back and forth across town, looking for girls. We hoped to visit some beauty, thinking she'd have friends to fix the rest of us up for the next dance. Breck was different from other private schools: we had no sister school. We had to find dates wherever we could. When Tim Hitchcock met a girl from Roosevelt, the next thing you knew someone from Breck was dating that girl's sister and two or three of us were lined up with other Roosevelt girls. We drove all over the place, trying to look cool in jeans, shirts with the little alligators, and penny loafers.

Once we had wheels a drive-in restaurant became an important destination. The "D.I." was our version of today's mall, or the Perkin's Pancake House of our kids' experience, except at the drive-in we were served in our cars. This was the place to hang out. The Lyndale Drive-In was the first in our neighborhood. A few blocks further on 61st was the Cottage where a bunch of girls from Holy Angels worked as car hops; they took your order and later brought a tray of food to hang on your window, loaded with Cokes, milk shakes, fries, burgers, and onion rings, all good stuff.

The girls at the Lyndale Drive-In were usually too busy to talk, or maybe they had too many guys bugging them. The Cottage was a little quieter and the girls had time to talk. Basically all the cars were filled with teen-agers, all hoping to pull in next to a car full of the opposite sex. On those perfect occasions when we got lucky and actually pulled in next to a few girls, an elaborate game of "Do you know?" would break out on the spot, interrupted only by taking time to give the carhop our order.

With all those kids coming and going, there was occasionally trouble. There were rules against wandering around, hanging out at someone else's car, undoubtedly to keep us from getting run over or having fights in the parking lot. On a rare occasion you could pretend to put something in your trunk and before getting back into your car you might slip the plastic ketchup bottle under the back of the front wheel. When you were ready to go, and your tray had been picked up, you could back out slowly and paint the car next to you a splash of red. By the time they figured out what had happened we were safely on our way, all pumped up, music blaring, the guys in back watching to see if we were about to be in a chase.

I was involved in just one car chase, with a relatively new Lincoln, driven by Joey Nelson, a guy who lived a block east of us on 46th and Dupont. The whole thing was touched off when Bobby yelled, "Joey, you got Daddy's car tonight!" as we passed them at a stop sign, intending to embarrass Joey in front of his buddies. We sped off in the other direction, but could see that they did a quick U-ie. Bobby and I were more than a little nervous thinking Joey and his friends might actually catch us and beat the tar out of us. It was like a short film, the two of us in my Pontiac, tipping around

Lyndale Drive-In, 5751 Lyndale Avenue South

corners, accelerating through the semi-darkness of an early summer evening, Bobby yelling directions and commentary on Joey's progress, our old beater followed by Joey and his friends in the Lincoln for a ten minute chase. We wheeled back and forth through the neighborhood before busting into the alley at 46th and Emerson. I had tangled with Joey once before, and only remember being kicked by his black engineering boot. He seemed intent on hurting me. We rumbled away down the alley as fast as I dared, cutoff open, reverberating off the garages on both sides.

"Can you see them?"

"Nice going, Rich. I think we just out-ran a nice new Lincoln."

I was relieved to not see Joey in the rear-view, chasing us down the alley with a boatload of his buddies. They should have caught us. We got away because Sherman had enough guts to complete the dodge, and we weren't afraid to bomb over the dip in the street to get into the alley.

Remember first base? It almost always happened in a car. Whether you were doubling, or whether you were driving your own car, the progression was the same. With my own car I could actually figure that out before taking the trip to the door after a date. We could talk. We could linger, try a couple of things, and see how it went.

If you were lucky to be dating someone—that meant you'd gone out with her more than once, preferably your next date was your third date, because that was when you and she were sure to be getting to the good part. The pressure was on. You both knew something was up, you had just kissed several times. Something was actually happening. You weren't sliding into second, but you were in the game.

When I was fifteen and we were beginning to drive I was an average, skinny adolescent, not bad looking, but I had some world-class pimples, and didn't know my ass from a hole in the ground about making out. There I was kissing Cindy Hanson in the back seat of someone's car. Things were getting good. Soon I would have something I could allude to…not talk about as such, but, yeah, we were kissing in the back seat. Nonchalant, Yeah. Or else there was the tickle route. A quick tickle as you move in a little, snuggle up, hold her arm so she couldn't tickle you back, and you had her.

O.K., now I was approaching first base. Not on first base, but getting close with a little kiss. I had no idea if the weak pop-up I just hit to shallow right would fall in for a hit, or "Adios." Back to the bench. But, guess what. I'm a teenage boy and it's my turn at bat.

A couple of kisses later, she's gotta go. Has to be in by 11:30. That's fine. That was nice. I bound out of the car to walk her to the door, and, we're not skipping to the door, but there's a little smile on my face. Things are definitely better. "I'll call you later this week. Maybe we can see a movie next weekend."

We'd get to the movie that next weekend in a '47 Pontiac, listening to the radio as we floated along, enjoying the ride, lurching occasionally as it did. Even after getting drummed out of the Glee Club because my scratchy little voice didn't have the range or tone for their snotty little group, I finally understood why all the popular songs of the day were about being with someone. They were all teenage love songs and were played on the car radio. If I weren't on a date right then, I might get one for next weekend. If not, I could always find a buddy or two to go bowling, maybe a movie, or hit the drive-in. At least now I had wheels. There were a lot of possibilities.

Porky's Drive-In, 1890 University Ave St Paul

Porky's Drive In

In the 1950s the American public renewed its love affair with the automobile. Vacation trips were now easier because of the expanding freeway system, cheap gasoline, and the growth of motel chains. Sedans gave way to two-tone cruising machines, complete with hood ornaments and chrome accenting. The new cars were "futuramic" in body and style.

Cars loaded with people were lured by the towering multi-colored signs at the roadside drive-in restaurants, which had become a part of the culture. It was a time of excitement and splendor where sharp cars and splashy signs met. The ties of image and identity between car and owner would become entwined forever.

The drive-in is where people came to eat and meet, while remaining inside or near their cars, which were their status symbols on four wheels. The food was fast and the atmosphere friendly. But most of all it was a place to be seen; find out who was with who and what was the local gossip.

The legendary Porky's Drive-In restaurant first appeared in 1953 on University Avenue in St. Paul and was followed by three more, two on Lake Street and one on Lyndale. At Porky's, the movement toward bold signage was taken to new heights by owner Ray Truelson. He made a garish black and yellow checked design on the first Porky's, the most eye-catching pattern to the human eye. He wanted people driving down the street to be literally forced to turn their heads because they couldn't help themselves. And it worked! After solidifying his reign as Twin Cities Drive-in king, Truelson later toned down those checks to red and white.

Porky's beacons called boisterously to the parade of vehicles on University Avenue. Customers studied the menu board and hollered their orders into a squawky box. The speaker system increased profits for drive-ins but not for carhops; eventually they were no longer needed. Porky's was a heavyweight among Twin Cities drive-ins where juicy hamburgers and deep-fried onion rings sparked the interest of classic car and hot rod enthusiasts. The Midway didn't really have anything until Porky's opened up, and it just became an instant hit. The Twin burger, Aunt Nora's fried chicken, malts and shakes were specialties on the menu. But the social part was what kept people coming.

For many years Porky's in south Minneapolis operated from a drive-in building near Lake and Calhoun. The structure was remodeled into Nora's Restaurant, which was remodeled once again into the upscale Tryg's.

Societal developments made it difficult for businesses

like Porky's to survive. As America slipped from the Fifties into the Sixties and Seventies, the drive-ins lost out to the chains. Zoning laws tamed the wild roadside, and the old drive-ins were suddenly out of date. One by one each closed or converted to sit-down restaurants.

In the early 1950s Ray Truelson had seen the future in a car; forty years later he saw it in nostalgia. In 1990 he re-opened the University Avenue Porky's, without the car hops this time around, but the hotrods were back, and so were the twinburgers and skin-on fries. He repaired the classic building and reopened the doors to fans of neon emblazoned drive-in architecture. Porky's was famous for its onion rings since the day it opened. When they reopened the onion rings were again made with the original Porky's recipe. Now car enthusiasts park their cars in Porky's lot for appreciative fans who admire the restored autos while enjoying a Porky's burger and fries.

Ray Truelson died in 1994, but Porky's still stands, a living roadside museum to a time when cruising the Avenue was a teenage way of life.

A&W ROOT BEER STANDS

The First Frosty Mug

One hot day in June of 1919 in Lodi, California, an entrepreneur named Roy Allen mixed up a batch of creamy root beer and sold the first frosty mug of this delightful beverage for one nickel. Now, more than seventy years later, A&W Root Beer is the world's number one selling root beer and is still mixed fresh daily and sold at hundreds of A&W restaurants.

Allen purchased the formula for his root beer from

a pharmacist in Arizona. To this day, the unique blend of herbs, spices, barks and berries remains a secret. With the success of his first root beer stand in Lodi, Allen soon opened a second stand in nearby Sacramento. It was there that what is thought to be the country's first "drive-in," featuring "tray-boys" for curb side service, opened up.

In 1922 Allen took on a partner, Frank Wright, an employee from his original Lodi location. The two partners combined their initials - "A" for Allen and "W" for Wright and formally named the beverage, A&W Root Beer. Three units were opened in Sacramento, then on to other northern and central California locations and the states of Texas and Utah.

Expanding the Chain

By 1933, the creamy beverage was such a success that there were more than 170 franchised outlets operating in the Midwest and the west. To insure uniform quality for the namesake beverage, Allen sold A&W Root Beer concentrate exclusively to each franchise operator.

During World War II no new restaurants were opened and despite governmental sugar rationing and employee shortages, most A&W units remained successful. After the war, the number of A&W restaurants tripled as GI loans paved the way for private enterprise to flourish.

In 1950, with more than 450 A&W restaurants operating nationwide, founder Roy Allen retired and sold the business to an aggressive Nebraskan named Gene Hurtz, who formed the A&W Root Beer Company. The post war era, the rapidly recovering economy and the popularity of the automobile provided the right environment for Hurtz's company to prosper. Drive-ins were becoming increasingly popular and A&W had the privilege of being one of the few nationally established drive-in restaurant chains. By 1960 the number of A&W restaurants had swelled to over 2000.

Bridgeman's

Bridgeman's began selling ice-cream cones in drug stores in 1936. Decades later, "meet me at Bridgeman's" was a call to indulge in contests to see who could eat the biggest sundae. A Twin Cities mainstay, Bridgeman's became famous for serving an ice-cream extravaganza called the Lalapalooza.

The Bridgeman's name stirs up fond memories for the people of the Midwest. Memories of grandma and grandpa taking you to Bridgeman's for a Sunday afternoon treat. Picking up an ice cream cone to enjoy on a walk. Meeting your friends for malteds after the big game. The story really goes back much further than this!

Back in 1883 in Duluth, Minnesota, an enterprising young man named Henry Bridgeman began peddling fresh milk house to house from a goat cart. Through persistence, hard work, quality products, and a little luck, his business grew into the largest dairy concern in the Midwest.

His sons, Chester and Roy Bridgeman, decided to strike out on their own. They opened the first Bridgeman's Ice Cream Shoppe in 1936. The venture was met with disbelief. Why would anyone open an ice cream shop in Minnesota? The climate wasn't right! What about the Depression? Chester and Roy heard the skeptics but they would not be stopped. They opened not one but six ice cream shops within eighteen months.

Since those early days the Bridgeman's name has been synonymous with high quality premium ice cream, fabulous ice cream treats, and superior service and cleanliness. A Co-branded Bridgeman's Ice Cream Shoppe allows a business to share in this hard-earned reputation, in a name that customers know and respect. Many of the Bridgeman's restaurants started out as drive-ins.

Carl andCarolyn Cederberg, Betty and Roger Kieley, all dressed up, 1965

Chapter 7

PUT ON YOUR GLOVES LET'S GO DOWNTOWN

Going Downtown with My Sister

My sister and I always began a shopping day by dressing up and walking over to Grand Street to catch the bus to ride downtown to Nicollet Avenue. I was between eight and twelve years old during those years when she took me with her. Often, I agreed to go only after she'd offered me some kind of bribe. Usually she would say, "I'll buy you a new shirtwaist." These were the most popular dresses of the times. Styled like a shirt and gathered at the waist, it was belted and had a full skirt with crinoline beneath. She knew I couldn't resist.

Taking the bus downtown was an experience. We'd cut through our neighbor's yard that was across the alley from us. I always felt strange doing it, but we were careful to walk strictly on the sidewalk and not harm Mrs. Warhol's well-tended tulip garden. Then, we'd walk to the bus stop, which was at the corner in front of an empty building that used to be a dress shop. I remember the bus costing a dime or quarter, but for a while we used tokens. You could get a deal by buying six tokens for a dollar.

The most exciting part of the trip was when the bus would vibrate and hum as we cruised over the Third Avenue Bridge. Looking down at the water was awesome and scary at the same time. It was so high you could see all the bridges downriver and also got a wide view of the city. Our family had moved from a small farming com-

Three Sisters women's clothing store, 6th and Nicollet, 1937

munity and I hadn't traveled much, so this was quite a thrill. I remember looking at the skyscrapers across the river. During Christmas the excitement was heightened when the city became especially festive, as new-fallen snow glistened on the lighted trees and church bells rang in the distance. Christmas carols were piped out on Nicollet Avenue and in the bus shelters.

We didn't have much money to spend as we came from a large family, but it was fun looking at the multitude of items for sale along the mall. It was a fast trip, as my sister would whirl me from store to store to shop, though I would like to have done more window-shopping, ogling the beautiful displays and examining the figurines and trinkets in the dime stores. I was always more of a dawdler and dreamer than she was.

We usually went to Penney's and Donaldson's and sometimes to Dayton's basement, where you could get some really great buys. Grayson's and Three Sisters were much more affordable and you could get even more stuff. Even into the 1970s, you could buy a blouse for $1.99 at Grayson's. We rarely went to Powers or Young Quinlan as those were higher-priced stores. I was fascinated that Young Quinlan had an elevator inside it, complete with operator, which stopped on the mezzanine.

My sister loved shoes, so we would spend a lot of time at Bakers, Burt's, Berlands and Chandlers, where she would try on lots of shoes. She was working at the phone company then and wore expensive dresses to work, and she tried to match her shoes with her outfit. Tie blouses, mohair skirts with jackets, and beautiful shifts of wool and knit were her favorites. It was a treat to go inside the shoe stores, as salesmen would greet us with a smile and measure our feet. Then, they would try to sweet talk and charm us into buying all kinds of accessories, like nylons and shoe polish, because they worked on commission. When we passed the Foshay Tower, once the tallest building in the Twin Cities, I got dizzy looking up. On the way home, the bridge and all the downtown buildings would be lit up.

History of Downtown Stores

From one store to the biggest mall in the USA

Shopping started in Minneapolis in 1848 when a store on old Main Street in St. Anthony was built. The G.W. Hale Dry Goods Company opened as the first department store on Nicollet and Washington Avenues in 1867, and moved in 1908 to Nicollet and Eighth Street. Other shops selling basic supplies such as tea, clothing and fishing tackle soon joined it. The first commercial district occupied the junction of Hennepin and Nicollet Avenues and was called Bridge Square.

Eventually, Nicollet Avenue flourished as the prime-shopping street, housing the largest and most esteemed department stores such as Donaldson's Glass Block, Dayton's, Powers, JC Penney's and Young Quinlan. (Elizabeth Quinlan had made history as the first woman clothing buyer.) As the city grew, so did the shopper's needs. The first enclosed mall in the world, Southdale Center, opened in 1956. Other malls soon followed in suburban settings. Downtown retailers stewed about losing revenue and came back with a recourse, which was a network of above-the-street, covered skyways, built in 1962 to connect the downtown blocks together.

In early times the business interests of the city had deliberately chosen to run streetcars on Hennepin and Marquette avenues but not on Nicollet Avenue itself. This enabled Nicollet to promote its safety and convenience for shoppers and secure its dominance as the city's primary retail street. In 1967 the city took the further step of turning Nicollet Avenue into a pedestrian mall, restricting vehicular traffic to taxis and buses and installing benches, planters and heated bus shelters.

Young Quinlan

Elizabeth Quinlan, 1948

Back in the early twentieth century, visitors to Minneapolis insisted upon seeing two places of interest: Minnehaha Falls and Young Quinlan's. Merchants in the east would say, "Minneapolis? Oh, yes... the home of the Young Quinlan store. Tell us, how does it happen that a store selling such fine things can thrive in that North Country?"

It was 1894 that a couple of young clerks from Goodfellow's, Fred D. Young and Elizabeth C. Quinlan, who had dreamed of starting their own business, decided to take the biggest risk of their lives and open a store that sold fashionable, ready-to-wear clothing for women. In those days, women sewed their own clothing or had tailors make their garments to order, so selling high fashion in ready-to-wear was truly a daring enterprise. There was only one such shop in the United States at the time in New York City. Minneapolis was merely a town on the edge of the prairie. How could a ready-to-wear shop thrive out in the "sticks"?

Young and Quinlan borrowed some money and opened their shop under the name of Fred D. Young and Company, in a room in the rear of Vrooman's Glove Shop in the Syndicate Building on 513 Nicollet Avenue. By the end of the first day they had sold out of everything. With Young handling most of the administrative work and Elizabeth concentrating on buying and selling, the shop grew. Within a few years, they had a full-fledged women's department store that fronted Nicollet Avenue. It catered to both the "carriage trade," which were wealthy women who came in horse-drawn carriages, and the Mainstreet trade. Miss Quinlan wanted the store to be more than a place where goods were sold. She knew the atmosphere that women enjoyed and succeeded in making the store into a desirable place for women to be together. Her store combined shopping in gracious and welcome surroundings with lunching out later.

Later when Fred Young passed away, Miss Quinlan was left to shoulder the responsibility of running the store alone. She was also faced with a decision of should she keep Young-Quinlan small, or attempt to expand the business? Quinlan decided to expand, but soon realized that she needed to learn more about merchandizing. She could not afford to make mistakes. But there were no schools or teachers of retail at the time, so she sought an audience with Gordon Selfridge of Marshall Field's, Paul Bonwit of Bonwit Teller's, Horace Saks, who later founded Saks' Fifth Avenue, Edward Filene of Filene's in Boston and B. Altman of Altman's in New York.

"From those master minds, I learned one lesson well," Miss Quinlan later remarked. "Always seek the best, whether it's in merchandise for the home or advice on business. Because the best is the least expensive in the end."

Quinlan broke new ground for a woman in business, as most store buyers were men. She made buying trips each year to Europe and, though at first reluctant to trust her own taste, she bought high fashions in small quantities. She brought back gowns from Paris, Berlin, Vienna and London. "But the most beautiful gown I ever sold was the creation of an American designer, Edward L. Mayar, a boy from Iowa who became world renown as a designer. It was a lace gown, beautifully cut, and edged in sable."

Whatever she selected sold well and her imports became trendsetters for the fashionable. Since ready-to-wear had consisted mainly of coats, capes, skirts and "wrappers," Quinlan introduced New York-made copies of Parisian suits having long skirts with three-inch trains and jackets with huge leg o-mutton sleeves. Women grabbed them eagerly. Then, Quinlan took the daring step of introducing ready-to-wear dresses. Hers was the first shop in America to carry them. Her fashions were not only sold to Twin City residents, but by mail to customers in Montana, the Dakotas, Iowa, Wisconsin, Michigan and Canada.

Miss Quinlan had two great ambitions. One was to build a business based on good quality and taste. The second was to be part of the civic life of a community and help those less fortunate than herself. In her mind, it was payment for the business the community was bestowing on her.

An elegant new store

In 1926, with the financial backing of the Rothschild's, Elizabeth Quinlan, along with William Lahiff, her nephew and general manager of the store, turned their backs on tradition again. They hired Frederick Ackerman of New York, an architect who specialized in homes, to build a beautiful new home for their merchandise emphasizing the austerity and simplicity of the finest Italian art.

The result was an elegant new Italian Renaissance-style building with five stories and a mezzanine. From the beautifully carved entrance to the sweeping grand stairway made of travertine, to amber cathedral windows, wide aisles, thickly carpeted and dotted with comfortable chairs and divans, the building was designed for relaxation and convenience. On the third floor was a fur storage vault with ammonia pipes that kept the temperature at freezing. On the fifth floor was a roomy auditorium, complete with stage, where fashion reviews were held. Some thought it resembled a women's club or elegant lounge.

Besides the beauty of the store itself, the new Y-Q included an entirely new feature… the first parking ramp of its kind in America, with spaces for 250 cars and an elevator going directly to the separate floors. The Minneapolis Tribune, on June 15, 1926, called the new building "a monument to a remarkable feminine achievement in a field supposedly dominated by men."

During the Great Depression, Franklin Roosevelt appointed Quinlan to the national board of the N. R. A. (National Retail Association), and before her death in 1947, she won recognition for her retailing innovations in both Time and Fortune magazines. The Young Quinlan Company went out of business in 1985, and Polo/Ralph Lauren now occupies the beautiful landmark building on Ninth and Nicollet.

(left) Street-level facade of Young Quinlan; (above) Fountain Tea Room, ca 1950.

A Long Time Favorite Gathering Spot: The Fountain Tea Room

When the Young Quinlan Department Store was closing its doors after 90 years, the patrons of the Fountain Tearoom were up in arms and started a petition to keep it open.

Every Monday through Saturday the tearoom was frequented by 200 to 300 people. Many had time for a leisurely lunch and some came every day. Most were elderly women with snow white hair shaped like perfect drifts. These women wore classic suits. Many were in furs.

Not that the tearoom was terribly expensive. For example, the classic salad of the week-- the chicken salad with toasted slivered almonds on pear halves, with a Strawberry Garnish, was $4.25. The most expensive item was the ever popular five french fried butterfly shrimp on toast for $5.25. The caramel rolls, known in Minnesota as "sticky buns" were 55 cents. The drink of choice was coffee for 50 cents. The owners didn't renew a liquor license so patrons could no longer get their Manhattans and Bacardi's for $1.85.

The busiest day was the third of the month, when Social Security checks were deposited. The food was good and easy to digest. The atmosphere pleasant. No dangling plants or loud music.

It was a doily kind of place. Doilies under the plates. Doilies under the glasses of Raspberry Crush made with raspberry sherbet smothered in fresh frozen raspberries and complimented with ice cold milk for $1.30. Chandeliers hung from the ceiling and the swan in the fountain spewed water over coins. Polite signs were posted in the area like: "Powder Room" and "Kindly signal for elevator."

The building was showing signs of aging but the customers didn't mind old and worn. Many would take the bus downtown for chicken salad at the Fountain Room even when the weather was below zero. Some of the ladies said they had been coming to the tearoom most of their lives. To break such a tradition seemed almost sacrilegious.

There was no chance the Fountain Room could stay open. But it was touching to see these elderly women doing their best to save it.

About 35 to 40 employees lost their jobs when it closed. Effie Lee had worked there for almost 23 years. Like many of the help, she did it all at the Fountain Room: smorgasbord preparer, baker, sandwich maker, pots and pans person - "everything in the kitchen." Some of her new people had been there five years, eight years. The salad girl had been there 20. There was a time when all the waitresses knew the customers. They were fond of the patrons, bustling around and asking, "And what can I do for you today?" and "How about a nice bowl of soup to warm you up?" Ina Stetson worked there one month short of 30 years. Helga Benson was one of the retired waitresses that often stopped in for lunch.

In 1985 The Ladies Who Lunch was a comedy put on by the AFOM Theater. The comedy spoof moved from farfetched to outlandish to bizarre, as the ladies schemed to block the closing of the Fountain Room. This play gave audiences a rare opportunity to enjoy performances by older women. The cast included Rose Schwartz, Jeri Dodge, Dorothy Crabb, Kay Hinz, Lillian King and Cecilia Larson. Many of these ladies attended fashion shows and had fond memories of the Fountain Room, a longtime gathering spot for Minneapolis's senior citizens.

Donaldson's Glass Block

Scottish immigrant Lawrence Donaldson joined his brother William and opened a single-story department store in 1882 at 310 Nicollet Avenue. Many businessmen shook their heads at the foolishness of the locality, wondering why they would put their store so far from the center of town. But the Donaldson brothers offered free transportation from the business area to the store and even set off gunpowder explosions on the roof to attract attention.

In 1888, they built the famed Donaldson's Glass Block, modelling it after French department stores. It was the city's first expansive store on the corner of Nicollet Avenue and Sixth Street. The principle attraction was the windows—more than in any other store in the city. It featured a total of fourteen departments devoted to goods with categories such as upholstery, boots and shoes, carpets, millinery, cookery, glassware and housekeeping. The store also had a complete lunchroom, which prior to that time had been attempted only by the biggest department stores out East. Donaldson's Glass Block was a turn of the century marvel; bringing a continental flavor to the cramped, dim retailing of that time. At night, the store lit up the skyline and in daytime, the dome on the corner of Nicollet and Sixth resembled the stores in Paris.

An ad for Donaldson's Glass Block in 1904 claimed they were fast becoming the clothing center of

Minneapolis and featured men's overcoats and suits. Children's Buster Brown suits and Russian overcoats sold for $4.98 as the Saturday Special and in the basement you could pick up a traveling trunk for $3.50 to $6.90. Other items for sale were phonographs on the fourth floor, Victor and Columbia talking machines, records and supplies. They also sold jewelry, candy, drug sundries, fall and winter footwear, and household necessities. The fourth floor Tea Room and Café served breakfast, lunch and afternoon tea for 25 to 50 cents.

When WWII came, Donaldson's did its part, dismantling the gray steel dome that had been its landmark, (built in 1888) and turned it into scrap. The old water pump in the basement, formerly used to furnish hydraulic power for elevators, was also dismantled for the scrap metal drive. Fifty tons of scrap were collected at the store for the drive in 1942.

During the years the two brothers operated the store, it made seven major expansions culminating in the construction of the eight-story building at Seventh and Nicollet. It was designed by the same architectural firm that had planned the Marshall Field's Store in Chicago, Selfridges in London, and Gimbals' in Philadelphia.

Donaldson's and Dayton's faced each other across the intersection of Nicollet and Seventh Street for most of the twentieth century. Donaldson's was older, but they both had a bargain basement and extended their stores into the suburban malls. In 1984 Donaldson's bought out six

From the Collections of the Hennepin History Museum

(above) Donaldson's Glass Block, 1925; (below) Donaldson's in 1950s.

Scenes from the Old Donaldson's

Powers stores and added them to the six stores they already owned.

The downtown Minneapolis building stood until 1982, when demolition began, but a fire unexpectedly finished off the remains on Thanksgiving Day of that year. The fire at Donaldson's spread to the Northwestern Bank nearby, destroying $90 million in property, and holds the distinction of the largest off-occupancy fire in the nation in 1982. The Saks Fifth Avenue wing of Gaviidae Common now occupies that block. Shortly after the fire, Donaldson's found a home across the mall in the City Center anchor spot until Carson Pirie Scott bought the company's stores in 1987. The downtown Carson's closed in January, and Montgomery Ward opened in a portion of that space in August of 1990.

Long Time Coffee Break

When an employee retires, she is entitled to unlimited coffee breaks. That was the saying that went around when three women retired, who had worked a total of ninety years together as waitresses in the Garden Room and the North Shore Grill at Donaldson's. Grace Hogevoll, Elizabeth Swanson and Floy Shackle were given electric coffee pots, a pound of coffee and a party to celebrate their service by their co-workers. All three said they had enjoyed their years of waitressing and had always treated their customers well.

Mrs. Shackle, who retired after 18 years, said her most embarrassing moment was when she poured coffee on a man's hand instead of in his cup. Mrs. Swanson, who retired after 37 years, spilled oyster stew on one of her customers and Mrs. Hogevoll remembered no embar-

rassing incidents as she had worked for the Donaldson's company for 44 years.

Daytons

George W. Dayton built his famous store on the corner of Seventh and Nicollet in 1902. He was originally a silent partner in the R.S. Goodfellow and Company, but it was not financially successful. Dayton found it necessary to buy out his partners and change the store name. Soon, he and his son Draper had the store on firm footing.

The store quickly became synonymous with quality merchandise, superior service, fashion leadership and community involvement. In 1969, the J. L. Hudson Company merged with Dayton's to form the Dayton Hudson Corporation, adding twenty-one Michigan stores to the nineteen they had in the upper Midwest.

Dayton's was the first American department store to establish a European buying office, which was located in Manchester, England. It was the first to open a dining room-style restaurant and offer a bridal registry. In addition, the store established many lines of exclusive private-label merchandise, including the world-famous Frango® chocolates and Boundary Waters clothing.

Each holiday season, Dayton's added to the festivities by its lavish store window displays that delighted young and old. These popular holiday traditions have been a part of Dayton's history for decades. The animated displays inside the 12,000 square feet auditorium in the downtown Minneapolis store have been a holiday tradition since 1963, with nearly 500,000 people viewing its presentations every year.

In June of 1990, Dayton Hudson acquired Marshall Fields. In 1991, Carson Pirie Scott sold their remaining stores to the Dayton Hudson Corporation (filed for bankruptcy and then in 1995, re-opened them under its moderately priced Mervyn's chain). In 2004, Target and The May Company announced its sale of the historic and respected Marshall Field's department stores, including the 62 stores serving communities in Illinois, Indiana, Michigan, Minnesota, North Dakota, Ohio, South Dakota and Wisconsin. Currently Macy's occupies many of the spots and continues the tradition of the eighth-floor Christmas displays.

Eighth Floor Auditorium

It started in the 1920s, when Dayton's put an animated elephant in their window display, which caused quite a commotion. It was their way of celebrating the holidays

The Nutcracker, Dayton's Holiday Show, 1973

in a big way. They used animated figures that featured real trees hanging outside the window and a wreath inside that was 40 feet tall.

The first eighth floor Christmas display was in 1966. The company turned the auditorium into a huge Charles Dickens Village, creating the London town scene with twenty different buildings that included antiques flown in from England. Of the150 different figures modeled to look like the characters in the novel, 109 of them were animated.

Every holiday season since then, a baroque display inspired by a fairy tale has been assembled on the eighth floor of the original Dayton's store. It's the Dayton family's annual gift to the community. Although the store has changed hands several times, people claim the show has changed very little over the years. Some say it has

SOME MEMORABLE
EIGHT FLOOR DISPLAYS

1966 Charles Dickens Christmas
1969 Peter Pan in Never, Never Land
1970 Charlie and the Chocolate Factory
1971 Babes in Toyland
1973 Nutcracker
1980 Alice's Wonderland
1981 Hansel and Gretel
1982 Pippi Longstocking
1986 Velveteen Rabbit
1988 Polar Express
1989 Cinderella
1991 Pinocchio
1992 Puss N Boots
1993 Beauty and the Beast
1998 Grinch Who Stole Christmas
2000 Harry Potter
2001 Snow White and the Seven Dwarfs
2002 Wind and the Willows
2003 Wizard of Oz
2004 Twelve Days of Christmas
2005 Santa Bear
2006 Mary Poppins

become even more elaborate. Colorful and whimsical vignettes are created by theatrical designers, three-dimensional animation combined with theatrical magic, and Fibre optics, while animated musicians play music scored by Minneapolis composers. Although many of the early displays were inspired by Disney themes, the later designs have relied more heavily on the creativity of fine art illustrators to define the look.

Year after year something about these displays manages to conjure up the same magic we felt as a young child, shuffling wide-eyed through a maze of bright lights and animatronics dreams. And even today you'll see young families, teenagers and older couples standing in a line that stretches all the way down to the elevators—proof that the Dayton family's gift has helped to define what a Minneapolis holiday, not to mention a downtown department store, should be.

The holiday auditorium exhibit usually attracts more than 400,000 annually. It takes a whole year to plan the event and it is open seven days a week from the first week in November to the end of December each year.

Santa Bear

This holiday teddy bear, a huge plush, white bear wearing a scarf and hat, was put on the market in 1985. The bear wore a different costume every year, and people began to collect them. At Christmastime people would decorate their homes with Santa Bear and include the stuffed animal in their holiday pictures. Santa Bear was becoming a Christmas mascot. The 1988 bear was fitted with a red satin tuxedo, red top hat, green bow tie, green cummerbund, and black and green walking stick.

With time Santa Bear's family grew to include his companion Miss Bear; baby Santa Bears, Santa Chop, a penguin, mouse and aggressive Bully Bear from the Santa Bear story line.

John Pellegrene was the driving force behind this run, which had its last season of sales in 2007 at the Macy stores. Pellegrene also brought Giorgio's fragrances and Boundary Waters merchandise to the Twin Cities. Hailing from Ohio, Mr. Pellegrene once considered becoming a clergyman. He has worked as a radio announcer and a tire salesman before coming to the Minneapolis Dayton's store, where he became the Senior Vice President of Marketing in 1984.

Holly Bell

Holly Bell became a Twin City institution on November 29, 1964 at the downtown Dayton store. Officials christened her "Holly" for the approaching season and "Bell" for her handy phone capabilities. There was a Holly Bell phone located on each floor of the store designed so that customers looking for an item could call and ask the location. A woman operator picked up the phone and always answered, "Holly Bell." It was a great service since the Dayton's store was huge

and during stages of remodeling merchandise often got moved around.

Holly answered an average of 800 to 1,000 questions a day: giving directions to visiting conventioneers, guiding pesky kids to the toy department, calling for emergency services, and directing people to the Oval Room to shop. She was a great source of information.

Teen Board

In high school there was probably nothing more prestigious than the Dayton's Teen Board. Thirty girls were chosen and introduced at the Back-to-School Style Show held in the Dayton's Sky Room. Twenty-six metro area public schools and four private schools were represented. It was a huge honor to be chosen as a Teen Board member. The one chosen had to be popular enough to spread new fashion ideas. She also had to look good in Dayton' clothing and keep up on the latest styles.

One of the most important duties of every Teen Board member was to be salesclerk in the Young Junior Department. Customers were reminded when buying clothes at

the downtown or Southdale location to give the name of their school, which would then be given credit. Therefore, the school and the Teen Board representative would be recognized for their effort.

A Teen Board member's other duties included planning school bulletin boards, editing monthly editions of the Teen Board's official news letter, the Teentonian. She would also be modeling in seasonal style shows—Back-to-School, Holiday, Easter and Graduation—and planning a style show for her classmates.

The girls got together again in September, greeting their peers at an "open house" held in the Young Juniors' Shop on the fourth floor that housed the headquarters for the Teen Board. The regular meeting day was the first Saturday of each month and the girls who assembled in the training department would hear talks about fashion trends, tips on selling and discussions for their future plans. The entire program was under the direction of Mary St. Clair of the Special Events Department.

Uniforms were chosen each year and worn by all thirty girls. The uniform for the 1960 school year had a skirt of black, white and brass pleats with a cotton blouse in a matching shade of brass worn under a black wool vest.

Board members advised classmates in the 1960 newsletter to wear culottes, knickers and knee-ticklers coordinated with a bulky sweater over the blouse, which was the perfect solution to the question of what to wear to that all-important Homecoming game. The newsletter described clothes and had pictures of students modeling them. Of course, all of the clothes could be purchased in the Young Juniors Shop at Dayton's. Make-up suggestions were also given. In the sixties, covering blemishes and freckles and keeping your lipstick as pale as possible were important suggestions. The Bobbie Brooks mix-and-match coordinates in plaids and pastels were very popular. As one member described a year of being on the Teen Board: it consisted of fittings, contests, new friends, beautiful fashions and was an experience no girl would ever forget. The J.C. Penney Company, Donaldson's and Young Quinlan also had teen boards.

Penney's Downtown Store

Hubert H. Humphrey bought his clothes at Penney's and so did many other Minneapolis mayors. Though there wasn't too much reaction when a movie star dropped by the cosmetic counter, when JC Penney himself showed up, people paid attention. He would come around just to see how things were going, even make a few sales. No one dared smoke around him because he was adamantly opposed to tobacco and drinking. When he was in the store, the washrooms would be guarded to make sure no one was smoking there, just in case he came by.

James Cash Penney had opened his first store in Kemmerer, Wyoming, in 1902, in a one-room frame building located between a laundry and boarding house. The store was furnished with makeshift counters and shelves made from packing crates. He and his family lived in the attic over the store. Penney clearly marked the price on every item in the store with "one price charged to all," regardless of what the customer's social status was. The practice was uncommon in those days.

Penney's store was "cash only," and local businessmen

predicted an early failure, but residents liked the merchandise and good service provided by the 27-year-old merchant, and Penney became an instant success. His deeper philosophical and religious beliefs became the credo of his business, and eventually hundreds of J.C. Penney stores were operating from coast to coast under the slogan "A Nationwide Institution."

In 1936, a Penney's store opened in the Andrus Building in downtown Minneapolis (later called Renaissance Square) on the southwest corner of Nicollet Avenue and Fifth Street. In 1952 the store moved across the street into the Syndicate Block building and was remodeled in 1959, with James Cash Penney himself cutting the ribbon for its grand reopening. At the time Penney had just introduced another shopping innovation—the department store credit card. The downtown store went out of business in June 1986 and in 1989, the building was torn down to make way for the Neiman Marcus wing of Gaviidae Common, an office tower and other buildings.

But during the 50s and 60s, the downtown Penney's store was thriving. The twelfth-largest of the sixteen hundred JC Penney stores operating at the time, it was nevertheless considered a family store that provided something for everyone, and was busy from morning to night. But as the suburban malls began to grow in the 1960s, the crowds at the downtown store diminished. Sales volume remained high but the company's earnings were beginning to drop. Shopping styles were changing.

When the downtown store finally closed in 1986, it was the end of a hundred years of dry goods retailing at that corner. Penney's salespeople fondly remember how

they had always felt like they were members of the Penney "family."

Earl Ewing sold shoes in the store for more than 25 years. He came from St. Joseph, Missouri, to settle in the Twin Cities in 1960. That was before the days of escalators, air conditioners and easy credit. When he started working there, salespeople collected only cash from their customers and the employees themselves were also paid in cash. Back then, men and women's shoes were all in the same department, and parents would come in with all the kids to get fitted and to talk about the old days and how things had changed.

Penney's has always stressed customer service and long-time customers often asked for Ewing personally. He admits that some customers were difficult. No matter what you did you couldn't please them, but you had to stick with them any way. Other customers were a dream—for example, the guy who liked a particular style of shoe so much he bought it in eight different colors, giving Ewing an easy sale of $200. In those days, Penney's had a casual atmosphere and it was not uncommon to eat a sandwich while you worked. At other times it was so busy you'd forget to eat lunch. Ewing retired when the downtown store closed and said that it was like leaving a place that was like home to him.

Doris Longerbone, another long-time employee, worked at the cosmetic counter, and she loved every minute of it—even the busy Christmas season, which is when she'd gotten her start as a temporary employee. After that Christmas, three girls left and she was asked to stay on and help. She ended up staying twenty-one years. She began to think of her customers as family and many of her regulars were wonderful people. They came in during the last week of the store closing just to say goodbye and give her a hug. They wondered sadly where they could get their Coty lipstick and compacts now. The other employees were like family to her, too. They were concerned with each other's families and lives. She said it was sad to leave the people and if the store hadn't closed, she wouldn't have left.

Another employee, Roselle Lavoy, worked at the Penney's downtown store for 25 years. Once, she chased a shoplifter nearly all the way to Hennepin Avenue though she was in her mid-sixties.

When the downtown store closed in 1986, JC Penney tried hard to absorb the 150 full-time and 50 part-time employees into their other stores. The building was demolished in 1989. It had been erected in 1885 and added to several times, the last addition coming in 1911. Nieman-Marcus's parent company, BCE Development,

bought the property and planned to build a retail and office project, including space for the IDS Financial Services. In 1989 and 1990 JC Penney was ranked as the top department store chain in the United States.

Powers

S. E. Olson was an immigrant from Rinusaker, Norway, who moved to Minneapolis in 1878 and went into the wholesale dry goods business with the house of N.B. Hardwood and Company. Hardwood lost his business in 1880, and Olson took the company's loss as his opportunity. He and another partner named Ingram were able to buy up "tail ends" from the wholesale business and set up a retail dry goods business for themselves which they called the Big Store.

During the early years Olson's store sold textiles, sewing supplies, and related items. In 1892, Olson secured a 100-year lease at the Lyman Tract property on the corner of 5th and First Avenue South, and later acquired some frontage on Nicollet Avenue, as well as the alley between 4th and 5th Streets. He erected an "arcade," which was an impressively large, ornate arched passageway that led into and extended throughout the store. In a few short years, Olson had built his business into one of the largest and finest department stores in the northwest.

Like several other prominent retailers, Olson made his mark not only through his business activities, but also by involving himself in city life. To protect the quality and atmosphere of downtown Minneapolis, Olson undertook actions to revoke a permit granted to the street railway company to lay tracks on Nicollet Avenue. Another example of his civic activity was in his initiation of the great Northwestern Exposition. He was also active in local politics and served on the staffs of three governors.

In 1901, Olson sold his business to a New York corporation, who installed Alonzo J. Powers as its president. Powers had worked at Field Leiter Dry Goods in Chicago (later to become Marshall Field) before coming to St. Paul to open a dry goods store with his brother. This business was in operation for more than 20 years before A.J. Powers took over the management of Olson's Big Store and reorganized it as Powers Mercantile Company.

Like his successor, Powers was alert to ways of expanding his business. In 1906, he leased property at the corner of 5th and Nicollet for the construction of a new, five-story, fireproof building; a deal which gave Powers a frontage of five lots on Nicollet Avenue. The Minneapolis Journal of September 22, 1906, reported this as a "transaction… of great significance to Nicollet Avenue and to Minneapolis." It established the permanency of the much-discussed property as a retail corner.

In 1937, the big department store was refaced on its entire street front of Nicollet and Marquette with cream-color Kasota stone. New display windows were installed and set in aluminate metal. A major factor in the remodeling was the belief that it would encourage other businesses on Nicollet Avenue to improve.

A hint as to the close-knit nature of Powers employees was when a woman's group called "Powers Old Women" was formed. No fliers were cir-

(top) Woman playing the organ above sales floor in Powers, 1951;
(bottom) Powers store at 417-429 Nicollet Avenue, ca 1937.

culated, no announcements made, no letters were sent. "We told one person about organizing the group and the next day we had two sheets of legal paper full of names." The company employed a welfare director regularly to look after the employees, as Powers felt it was his duty to encourage and promote their education, entertainment and enlightenment. Groups were formed such as the Loyalty League, Power's Men's Club, and a monthly publication was distributed called Hours at Powers. An employee newspaper was also created.

Roughly speaking, the merchandise at Powers was divided into four branches: men's, women and children's, grocery and meat, and house furnishings. The stock of dry goods was unsurpassed by any other local establishment. Lady shopper's could buy gloves, corsets, millinery, ribbons, jewelry, silverware, cut glass, silks and footwear for every member of the family.

Among the special features which set Powers apart was an outstanding book department under the management of Mrs. Alice Carlson that often obtained rare and valuable editions. The downtown store was also valued for its relaxed and comfortable atmosphere. There was a wonderful cafe downstairs where the homemade pies were heavenly. Powers was also noted for caring clerks and in later years, its innovative sidewalk cafe.

In 1963 Powers suffered a half-million dollars in damages during a fire, and it burned again in 1976 when fire spread from a neighboring building on the Nicollet Mall causing four million dollars in damages. In an attempt to keep step with the times, the Powers Dry Goods Company added six suburban locations, and in 1985 it was acquired by the Donald-

One yard skirt in one hour, 1949

son Company. The downtown store closed and the building was demolished. A parking lot now stands in its place.

Ending of Downtown Shopping Era

Until the day it closed its doors, Powers was considered one of the top three department stores in downtown Minneapolis, behind Dayton's and Donaldson's. Less than a year after it closed, J.C. Penney also shut its doors, and downtown Minneapolis found itself without a moderately-priced department store.

(top) Chandlers Shoes display window, 1955.
(bottom) Berland's Shoe Store, 709 Nicollet Avenue in Minneapolis, 1939

Chandler Shoes

In downtown Minneapolis during the 1950s and 60s there were 13 shoe stores. On a Saturday women had their pick and sometimes would choose to visit all of them and compared prices and styles. So many baby boomers remember Burt's, Bakers, Berlands, Chandlers, and Jaeffees shoe stores.

In 1922, six Edison brothers opened a shoe store called Chandlers. Although there was relatively little variation in footwear styles at that time, the Edisons' new store sold stylish women's shoes for six dollars. This one-price policy soon became an industry standard as other chains discovered that the practice increased sales.

The Edison brothers' father, a Latvian immigrant and all of the Edison sons had connections to footwear sales. The first store was an immediate success, with their low prices attracting customers from many markets, including the upper class. Growth was fast and furious and they opened a second store called Baker's that was geared toward an even lower-priced market. By 1928 the Edisons had a chain of twelve stores stretching across the United States. When the Great Depression hit they opened a new chain called Burt's, which sold a line of $2.88 shoes. Thus, the Edison Brothers were diversified and in fairly good shape compared to their competitors.

In the course of time the Edison Brothers expanded into apparel and virtuality software, and the company now owns and operates 1,883 apparel stores including J. Riggings, JW/Jeans West, and Oaktree; 766 footwear stores including Bakers/Leeds, Wild Pair, and Sacha London; and 138 entertainment units including Dave & Buster's, Time-Out, and Space Port.

Amluxen's

Fabric expert and manager George Amluxen III operated a fabric store on Nicollet Avenue for many years. He would buy tons of bolts in all different colors and display them on tables in the store, which bore his family name. Founded by his grandfather in the 1930s, son George Jr. also worked in the store. Grandson, George III, said he sort of "inherited" the job and found to his surprise he loved it.

"My grandfather taught me from the beginning that you can't do business from an empty wagon." That accounts for the huge inventory Amluxen's carried. "If we don't have exactly what a customer asks for, we can usually find a pretty close substitute," George III said. Amluxen's imported about half their materials. According to him, American materials were turned out so fast they were inferior and many times had flaws.

"We have an image to preserve. We try very hard to have all our merchandise first class. I personally like to work on the floor and talk to customers. That's the surest way to know what they like—or don't like. Of course we rely heavily on our old pros—our 75 employees who really know the stock and where to find it."

One of the pros in whom George Amluxen had great

Informal Modeling while you shop. Enjoy seeing the very latest fashions in velvety textured fabrics by Crompton

Thurs. Aug. 25th
913 Nicollet
12:00–5:00
Fri. Aug. 26th
Ridgedale
12:00–5:00
Sat. Aug. 27th
Southdale
12:00–5:00

amluxen's
quality fabrics

confidence was Mrs. Myrtle Smyder of St. Louis Park, who helped him with buying. They made several trips to New York annually to select fabrics. Mrs. Smyder knew a lot about patterns too and said the "new size" was giving more than one dressmaker problems. To neutralize some of those problems, the Amluxen Company started a sewing school in a building across the Mall at 920 Nicollet Avenue. Instruction was free if you bought the fabric at the store. A teacher was on duty all day, every day, and she personally helped sewers lay out patterns and later aided them with the final fitting.

Though none of them could match the downtown store, which had four floors of imported fabrics, by the 1970s Amluxen's stores had also opened at Southdale, Ridgedale, and Rosedale. These stores closed in the 1980s. Like other small fabric retailers, Amluxens suffered from dramatic changes in the home-sewing business that began in the mid 1970s. Until then, home-sewing had grown in popularity, not only because pattern makers kept the patterns simple, but also because double-knit fabrics had come to the market. As more women began working outside of the home, they had more money to buy clothes and less time to sew their own. Meanwhile, double-knits fell out of favor, and the industry went into a downturn. Large specialty chains such as Minnesota Fabrics began to do well, but the small independents were squeezed out of the market.

The George Am-luxen's lived in Edina. Mrs. Amluxen was a fan of sew-it-at-home herself. That's the way she met her husband as he waited on her when she came into the store to buy some fabric.

The Nankin Restaurant

The Nankin Res-taurant, which opened for business in 1919 at the corner of Seventh and Hen-nepin, provided the first taste of Chinese food for many Min-nesotans, and became a Minneapolis dining tradition. Advice from the 1933 menu was, "Chinese foods are famous for their balanced rations. More healthful than the heavy meat dishes that leaves one sluggish. For your health and pleasure, eat at least a few Chinese dishes every week." In those days no one could have guessed how much interest folks would eventually take in Chinese food.

For decades the Nankin's mufti-colored, orange pagoda-topped sign was a Minneapolis landmark, glowing like a mini Chinatown. It even made the ster-ile wall of the nearby three-level parking ramp look in-viting. In the early years a vaudeville theater had stood next-door, where in the '50's one of the waitresses had won a Liz Taylor look-a-like contest. The front bar served real old-time fancy drinks and martinis, like the bars did back then.

Working at the Nankin

Linda Herkenhoff

I was hired on the spot at the tender age of eighteen. The front of the store was fairly elegant for the day, especially the downstairs dining room. The back of the place was not--old concrete, stainless steel food stations. Nobody spoke English very well, or at least didn't let on that they did, and it was often difficult to ask questions or make sure they understood what you wanted. The back of the restaurant was very loud, with ceaseless chopping and people yelling orders out in Chinese. It was actually chaotic most of the time. I was a quiet, unassuming young woman and I had to start raising my voice and throwing food back across the counter.

I worked upstairs. The kitchen was mostly downstairs. If you had two dishes (they always came with a stainless heat cover) it was easiest to come up the back. If you had a tray full, you had to come up the front staircase. The staircase was kind of a showpiece for the restaurant, it was wide and red carpeted. If you went up in front you had to carry your tray over your shoulder one handed all the way up. It was one of the "rules". I almost lost a couple of dishes when I first started but one of the waiters caught my tray from behind and showed me how to do it.

We wore green cotton Geisha-inspired dresses for uniforms. They were light green with dark green piping that came up one side and crossed over the chest to button on the other side of a high tunic-like neck. They were form fitting but not tight. We wore white waitress/nurses shoes and our hair up if it was long. We were supposed to wear hairnets but nobody did unless someone complained, then we all wore them for a few days.

The upstairs where I worked was divided into five or six stations of four booths each. It was cozy. The rumor was that the younger women were hired for the upstairs because the manager was a pervert and was always ogling us and more. There were a lot of very pretty young women working upstairs. It turned out that the rumors were true, but even though it was reported many times by staff, nothing ever happened to him.

The lower level was more open. The second story looked over the main room, balcony-style, so the front part of the main floor had very high ceilings. It was kind of dark, decorated with lots of red—lanterns and dragons—but done tastefully. It seemed the kind of place you'd meet your friends for lunch or a fancier restaurant where people would go before an evening show. Lots of the evening crowd were dressed up.

Everyone raved about the food. Even if someone hadn't been there in years they seemed to have fond memories of what they'd had last time they were at the Nankin. Unless they had more than two "wanderer's punch" drinks.

The popular Nankin eventually outgrew its dark and cozy dining rooms and in 1958 Carl Chalfen, Morris Chalfen and Sam Golden bought it and moved it across the street. After Sam's death, Carl and son Joel owned the restaurant together.

The imaginative new space featured a grand staircase that led to a picturesque balcony with tranquil Asian paintings hanging on the walls. The lanterns, though new, were duplicates of the ones that had hung in the old building.

When the City Center developers began construction of the 32-story Amfac-City Center Hotel and Scotties Restaurant, they delayed tearing down the Nankin to minimize the length of time the restaurant would be closed down.

The Nankin moved a third time into a huge new space on Hennepin Avenue, equally attractive in decor. On the final closing day thousands of admirers came to order the Nankin specialty, Sub gum Chicken Chow Mein, which may have been the most frequently ordered meal anywhere in the Midwest at that time. It was said that the Nankin was responsible for the Twin Cities having so many good Chinese restaurants, because most of the cooks who started at the Nankin went on to launch their own restaurants.

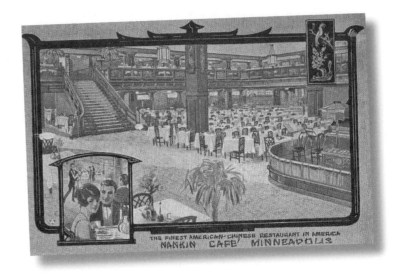

THE FINEST AMERICAN-CHINESE RESTAURANT IN AMERICA
NANKIN CAFE MINNEAPOLIS

My Own Memories of the Nankin

I remember our whole family going to the Nankin in downtown Minneapolis when I was very young, just after we moved here in 1956. It was still the original Nankin then, and the first Chinese restaurant in the Twin City area, so it was a unique place to go. And when you consider that our family had barely ventured into town from the farm at the time, and seldom went to restaurants of any kind, this was truly a sensory experience.

We were a large group. I was escorted, along with my mother and my eight brothers and sisters and some of their spouses, into an octagonal-shaped booth with silk room-dividers that surrounded the table, which made our meal seem more private. To a child from a small town, the Nankin's exotic decor seemed magical: colorful, delicate Chinese lanterns drifting above our heads, soft avocado-green and orange woodwork cut in traditional oriental curves and angles, an ebony and brass shrine gleaming above the doorway, and in the entranceway two statues of elderly Chinese people dressed in golden robes. Live turtles swam in a penny-lined wishing pond.

The sweet smell of Chinese food hung in the air and welcomed us in. We were served wonton soup in white bowls and later came the intrigue of opening the message inside a fortune cookie. But, the most memorable part of the meal for me was the weak sugared tea that was served in thick china cups with no handles and stamped on the side with crimson and emerald dragons. The waitress kept filling our cups from a white teapot decorated with turquoise and coral flowers, and I kept emptying mine. I think it was to be sipped, but instead I gulped it down. I loved this sugary water, as it was a grown-up drink that I had never tasted and the elegance of the tiny cup made it seem more exotic.

The Forum Cafeteria

Wherever you came from, whatever your background... at the Forum you were eating lunch in style! In the 1930's, the grand Strand Theater closed and later renovated to have this wonderful old building become home to the Forum Cafeteria. The Strand's seductive nineteenth-century Romanesque façade invited you inside with its flashing exterior lights. The interior shimmered with classic art deco design as green glass partitions etched with zigzags and jagged-shaped patterns divided the tables. Frost-ed-glass chandeliers cascaded overhead and silvery mirrors hung on walls. Scenes of Twin City lakes and neighborhoods were hand painted on the walls in extravagant style.

On the other hand, the cuisine was typical dinner fare. Chicken pot pies were a signature Forum lunch item offered daily in the 1950's. Dinner choices were standbys of the era—we call it comfort food today—such as baked ham, fried chicken with milk gravy, stuffed pork cutlets, Swiss steak, pot roast with gravy and dressing, and stewed chicken and dumplings. The Forum was open from 6 a.m. to 9 p.m. seven days a week, where inexpensive dinners were served cafeteria style. In 1956, full dinners were under a dollar.

For more than forty years, countless diners lined up to eat and admire the glass lighting, smoky sensuality and ambience that was a lot like the old vaudeville theaters. In 1972, the beautiful exterior was dismantled and placed in storage. The Historic Preservation Commission protects the art deco etched glass, tile and mirrors in the interior today, and the building is listed on the National Register of Historic places. After the Forum closed, it became a nightclub called Scotty's On Seventh from 1982 to 1992, and remained open as Goodfellow's Restaurant until 2000.

Memories of Downtown and Working at the Forum

Betty Kieley

When I was in third grade I would take the streetcar downtown with my sister Carolyn or friend Gerri. We would buy our school clothes at either Lerner's or Three Sisters on the Nicollet Mall. Dayton's Basement had fabrics, millinery and notions, and we would also shop at that great fabric store called Amluxen's on ninth and Nicollet. In sixth and seventh grade, we made pleated summer skirts out of pastel gingham. In high school, if you bought shoes from the Oval Room it was prestigious to carry the box that had a special carrying handle.

We loved going down to the Radio City Theater on Ninth and LaSalle. It was a beautiful building. The Metropolitan was another beautiful building with ornate steps. Both buildings have since been torn down. What a shame! When a group of us wanted to go downtown on a Saturday for an afternoon of fun, we would see a movie, go to Bridgeman's for a turtle sundae, then to the library to look at the mummy. We would be scared and laughing at the same time. We didn't like the mummy, but somehow we were drawn to it.

In seventh grade I had my first pizza, served by the slice from the dime store. I didn't like it at first. There were lots of shoe stores downtown and that's where I met my husband, Roger. He was working at Berland's.

In tenth and eleventh grade, I got my first job at the Forum. I was too short to serve customers so I was the water girl and did clean up. We had to wear a hair net and a gray and white starched uniform with an apron. I remember after getting the job I was told to go downstairs where a seamstress measured me and hemmed my uniform. That was in 1959.

On Sundays after church, we always went out for lunch. We went to either the Forum or Harts in Wayzata. At the Forum we had a meat patty with gravy, French fries and chocolate pudding every week.

Later, I got a job at the phone company where I worked through high school. I continued to work there after I was married and had my first child. I worked as an information operator with a line of other girls. We had a crabby supervisor that watched everything we did.

Shopping Downtown

Mary Dymanyk

We used to dress up in our hats and nice dresses to go downtown. Donaldson's second floor had the nicest and biggest variety of housedresses. I remember going to Woolworths and buying a bag of candy in the front of the store that was weighed and sold by the pound. Also, there were nuts displayed in a glass case and served warm. I loved to look at the canaries.

Donaldson's had a long lunch counter and so did Powers. They were right next to each other. We used to shop at Dayton's basement where you could get bargains. The lunch counter there was called the Grille. We loved to look at the window displays that were always so unique. There were two Chinese places you could get ChowMein—John's Variety and one on Hennepin Avenue. We also liked going to the Forum, which served inexpensive food cafeteria style. Fanny Farmer was a great store and unique at the time. Movies during the week after work were cheaper. Then, we'd go to Bridgeman's for a Hot

Fudge Sundae or Triple Treat.

I bought a coat in 1954 at Young Quinlan. It was gray wool and Princess style. I loved that coat. The elevator would stop at the mezzanine and was operated by a real person. Second floor was ladies house-wares.

I remember working at Dayton's for the Christmas holidays when I was still in high school. Students with good grades could work at Dayton's as extra workers. We got another week off of school then. Dayton's treated their workers special. If you worked late, you got your supper for free. You received a Christmas bonus, even if you only worked for two weeks. I worked in the mail order room.

I also have fond memories of taking my nieces and nephews downtown every year. They could pick out whatever they wanted for a gift. We would go off in different directions in the toy department and I didn't have to worry about them. Then, we'd eat at a huge cafeteria or at Woolworth's Second Floor of the IDS. It was a big deal for them to go to the top of the Foshay Tower and look out over the city. Then, we'd take the streetcar or a taxi home.

Parade in front of Woolworths, 1959

Chapter 8

DIME STORE DREAMS

One of the popular pastimes of the Sixties was to go to the five and ten cent store, or as we used to say, "The dime store." Most of us remember Grants, Woolworth's and Kresge variety stores. The best modern likeness to them is the abundance of Dollar stores that have popped up in strip malls all over the place.

Dime stores didn't put every thing on shelves and racks like they do today at the local Wal-Mart. Everything was placed on top of counters. Gaily-colored packages, guaranteed to attract a child's eye, might contain a pink jump rope, toy jacks or a bag of cat's eye marbles. Inside other packages were things I could only dream about as I passed by with my sister. I especially loved the sets of toiletries for young girls that had pink bottles of toy lipstick, nail polish and tiny bottles of toilet water inside. Rows and rows of hair items—combs, brushes, hair ribbons, bobby pins and barrettes—hung in packages on hooks. As I wandered through the store, completely forgetting the moment, I would be transported to another time where little girls could walk on paths of rose-colored petals wearing gaily colored dresses, lacey anklets and patent leather shoes.

Shopping usually started in the 600 block of Nicollet Avenue in downtown Minneapolis where the W. T. Grant store was located. Kresge's was right next door, and Woolworth's was the next block down at 701 Nicol-

let Avenue. I liked looking at all the knickknacks, figurines and decorations each store had for every holiday. It wasn't just the toys, but all the shiny, colorful objects that caught my eye, and the way they were displayed.

But the best part of the store was the lunch counter or luncheonette (as it was called back then). I would sit on top of the stool and spin around while my sister ordered two grilled cheese sandwiches and Cokes. The sandwiches were fried until the cheese had melted and the bread had taken on a golden hue, and then cut into four small triangles and placed on a plate with a pile of potato chips in the center. The cokes were in real glasses with crushed ice, and there were two straws per person.

Kresge's had a tall counter where you could eat a cheap lunch of single-sliced pizza or perhaps a hot dog served with grilled bun, seared just right and placed inside a small accordion-folded carton. No one else served hot dogs like they did. It was the best place in town to take a break from shopping and go inside for just a Coke or browse through all the neat stuff. The place was always packed with customers and it was hard to get a seat during lunch.

Kresge's

This discount variety store, which opened in 1929, was among the first to introduce speedy new checkout counters in the 1950s. The Luncheonette was in the basement of the store. The second floor featured sewing notions, fabric and housewares. The main sales floor included candy, stationery and albums. A five-alarm fire destroyed the building on November 12, 1968, and rather than build a new store, Kresge sold his location (which is now part of the City Center block) to IDS Properties and concentrated his attention on his suburban chain known today as K-mart.

S. S. Kresge

Sebastian Spering Kresge worked as a traveling salesman and sold tin ware for seven years before he opened a discount retail store whose merchandise was priced at less than a dime. He opened his first store in downtown Detroit in 1899, going into business with J. G. McCrory, who owned a chain of stores in the northeast part of the United States. Together, they opened many stores. In 1912, Kresge bought out McCrory and incorporated himself as S. S. Kresge. At the time the chain included 85 stores, the largest of which was in downtown Kansas City. By the mid-1920s, the S.S. Kresge Company was opening new locations that sold items for $1 or less, a precursor to the current discount store.

With a strong religious upbringing, Kresge was a thrifty, caring person. To commemorate the 25th anniversary of his company, he established The Kresge Foundation in 1924 through an initial gift of $1.3 million. By the time of his death at age 99 in 1966, Sebastian Kresge had made additional gifts totaling over $60 million.

Exterior (left) and lunch counter of the S.S. Kresge Store at 628 Nicollet Avenue in Minneapolis, 1958.

Easter window display (left) and doll counter at W. T. Grant store, 1957.

Grant's

Grant's, another discount variety store was located on the current City Center block. It opened in 1929. The original building was also home to the Allen Shoe Store, Holly Dress Shop and a dry goods store, which gave Grant's a certain renown for being four-stores-in-one. In 1955 the old six-story, red brick building was turned into a streamlined new version of enamel and granite highlighted by stainless aluminum doors and a show of windows. A forty-four-stool luncheonette with conveyor belt was among the special features of the new store, which also included many specially designed "shop-at-a-glance" counters with display fixtures. The floor-space inside the new building was more than double that of the original building. On the first floor were the luncheonette, candy, jewelry, notions, toilet goods, hosiery, infants and children's, women's wear, knit underwear, stationery, leather goods, the millinery department and dress shop. The downstairs store included men's accessories and the boy's department, yard goods, drapery, shoes, grocery, hardware, electric, home furnishings, rugs, furniture, toy department and pet shop. Grant's closed in 1970 and the Woolworth store temporarily filled its spot.

W.T. Grant

With a $1,000 investment, William T. Grant founded the Grants Company in 1906. The store was first located inside the Lynn, Massachusetts Young Men's Christian Association building. A sign in the window on opening day proclaimed, "A new kind of store—a department conscious shoppers turned to lower and lower priced stores. But by 1940, Grant had begun to introduce high-ticket items like furniture and appliances, and to open new stores in the emerging suburbs. Thus muddled the image for some older shoppers who remembered the old variety store and still expected bargain-priced goods.

In the 1960s, Grant virtually showered credit cards on all his customers and gave his employees bonuses for signing up new credit card customers. In 1969, Grant opened 28 stores, but earnings had already peaked in 1966 and now they began to sag. The downtown Nicollet store was closed in 1975.

Woolworth's

Woolworth's opened its first store in downtown Minneapolis in 1920 at Third and Nicollet. In 1936, they constructed an art deco building on the southeast corner of Seventh and Nicollet. In its heyday, Woolworth's competed with Grant's, Kresge's and even JC Penney's. All of these stores catered to middle- and low-income shoppers. The building was demolished in 1973 to make room for the IDS Center and Crystal Court, which left a three level corner space for Woolworth's along with several restaurants.

F.W. Woolworth

In 1879, Frank Winfield Woolworth created a retail chain store that offered wide selections of merchandise at reasonable prices. The Five Cent Store filled an unmet need, but not on famous brands and high quality. At Woolworth's everyone felt rich because they could buy anything they wanted.

W.T. Grant store, 604 Nicollet Avenue in Minneapolis, 1954

store with nothing over 25 cents." Grants merchandizing inspiration was to fill the niche between the burgeoning "five-and-dimes" and the department stores, whose wares at that time began at around 50 cents. With the emphasis on solid quality at bargain prices, the Grant chain expanded.

The Great Depression was a time of further expansion and prosperity for the variety store chains, as budget-

Sixteen-year old Frank Woolworth had left the farm he grew up on to work for Augsbury and Moore's Dry-goods. He worked for them three months without pay. Though not a strong salesman, he did have a creative knack for displaying merchandise in store windows. His arrangement of a display of cut-rate items with a sign that read, "Anything on this counter 5 Cents" became so popular that his boss suggested he open a store devoted entirely to nickel goods. He opened his first store in Utica, New York, but it was not profitable. His Lancaster, Pennsylvania store became a great success.

For more than a century the familiar red and gold mastheads, with their popular red striped awnings, dotted main streets throughout the United States and Canada. Woolworth's later expanded into England, Germany, and Cuba. During the centennial in 1979, the Woolworth Company owned 4,000 general merchandise and specialty stores and employed almost 200,000 employees. Specialty stores were the Woolco Department Stores, Kinney Shoes and Richman Brothers Men's and Baby clothing.

Woolworth's:
Memories of a Downtown Landmark

The store moved into the former Grant's space while waiting for a new home, then cut ribbon on a 90,000 square foot store in the IDS Center. Its Harvest House Cafeteria was decorated in red, with Tiffany glass panel partitions between the booths. Their specialty foods were strawberry pie, German chocolate and lemon-layer cake, and all-you-can-eat fish or chicken. Woolworth's was one of the last places where you could get a meal with good mashed potatoes and gravy. Off the skyway to Dayton's was the Quiet Corner Coffee Shop that was decorated in green, black and yellow-check seat cushions and curtains.

The Concourse Grill was at the store's basement level.

During the heyday of downtown shopping, Woolworth's was more than a store. It was an institution, with plenty of bargains and several restaurants that were always busy. When the downtown Woolworth's store closed in 1993, it left many people wondering what was the point of coming downtown. Some said the store was a haven and even the soul of downtown. People had been drawn by its senior citizen specials and values the familiarity of a store they had grown up with could offer. Office workers from the IDS had stopped by for coffee breaks and to smoke. Regulars had come to eat, shop, meet with friends, and catch up on community gossip.

Many elderly shoppers were in the habit of starting their day at Woolworth's with a cup of coffee at the cafeteria, and having another one before heading home at the end of the day. They'd stop for a long lunch as they shared the dining room with office workers and also homeless people. So many depended on the old-line variety store for convenience, affordable goods and meals. Especially hurt when they closed down were the city bus riders, many of whom couldn't afford to shop elsewhere. Evelyn Hass, Alice Saice, Dixie Omites and Rita Bartos were once waitresses at Woolworth's. They had to find other jobs after working there for many years.

Pet Department

Many Minneapolis Baby-Boomers have fond memories of Woolworth's Pet Department, where they went when they were young to buy parakeets, turtles, gold fish, hamsters and baby chicks—sometimes with their own money! Kids loved the pet department, but it caused problems for employees as parakeets would escape and fly all over the store, sometimes dive-bombing the customers at the lunch counter. Calamity ensued when hundreds of hamsters at a Woolworth's store in Ohio escaped, got into the ceiling, and started chewing the wiring.

Candy Sold by the Pound

Another fond memory I have of the Woolworth's store is of the counter where candy was displayed on glass trays that spun around on lighted carousels. The aroma and sight of chocolate would lure people into buying a quarter of a pound to sample while they shopped for other things. In fact, back in 1886, Frank Woolworth was the first retailer to sell candy in bulk. After some test marketing, he offered Operas, Montevideo's, Nougatines and Vanilla Caramels at 5 cents for each quarter pound. Before long, candy had become one of the most popular features of Woolworth's, especially during the holidays. Handpicked candy clerks carefully weighed candy on

Photo Machines

O ne great memory I have about Woolworth's was taking pictures in the photo machine, which gave you four photos for twenty-five cents. A group of friends and I would pile into the booth after school, insert a quarter, then close the curtain and start posing. But we had to act quickly as every 15 seconds a flash would go off and everyone would have to start making new faces. After several minutes, developed pictures would fall out of the slot. We were thrilled at how cheap and easy it was to preserve our memories. We would often exchange these photos with our friends. Although they had been taken on cheap film and printed on cheap paper, they lasted for many years.

scales, then placed them inside paper bags. Hot roasted peanuts, popcorn and fudge were added to the variety later. Candy counters became the busiest place in the store.

Chewing Gum

One of the biggest boosts to Woolworth's candy business was chewing gum. Gum had been around since the Civil War, but didn't become really popular until 1914. In 1919, Woolworth's earned an income on its sale of 14 million packages of gum. Some of the early favorites were Beeman's, Black Jack, Juicy Fruit and Clove, which was believed to cover up the smell of tobacco on one's breath.

Teenagers

Many teenagers found Woolworth's to be a great place to go for their needs. You could buy a tube of lipstick or a stack of 45 RPM records to play and trade with your friends or just a poster of a favorite movie star. For a long time records were 25 or 35 cents. You could find just about everything in the store—even romance. Lots of young couples first met at the Woolworth's lunch counter, a favorite place to hang out.

Lunch Counters

When the first restaurant at Woolworth's opened in 1910, nothing on the menu cost more than 10 cents. Up until World War II, you could get a complete meal for a quarter. Many food items were tried and proven unsuccessful, until ice cream cones were test-marketed in larger cities. The treat caught on quickly, along with serving root beer and hot dogs at lunchtime. Root beer was drawn from an oak barrel on the counter. This brought in even more customers. The idea was if the customer didn't have to leave the store for lunch, they would shop longer.

The first full-scale restaurant in a five and dime store was in New York. The "Refreshment Room" featured glass-top tables and a forty-foot glass lunch counter. It served oysters as Roth's orchestra played the Woolworth March and other popular songs such as "Let Me Call You Sweetheart" and "Shine on Harvest Moon." Woolworth's opened many restaurants across the country. By 1928, the stores were serving 90 million meals a day. After World War II, lunch counters and luncheonettes replaced most of the lavish Refreshment Rooms; the counters were made of Formica. The company started to introduce in–house promotions such as Banana Splits, Turkey Days, Vegetable Week and Dairy Month. Specials depended upon what the area farmers had a surplus of.

In the 1970s, before fast food restaurants became numerous, Woolworth's bakeries and luncheonettes were often the only places you could go to get reasonably priced food with fast service. There were stand-up counters, sit-down counters and cafeterias as well as bakeries and soda fountains in almost all of the Woolworth stores.

Woolworth's busy lunch counter, 1956

The volume of food served made Woolworth's one of the largest suppliers of prepared foods. Millions of burger patties, cheese slices, potatoes, bananas and Maraschino cherries were served. Eating at Woolworth's on a Saturday afternoon became a tradition for many.

A Long Counter

By the '40s and '50s, in-store dining had returned to the Midwest in the form of a full-service lunch counter. Customers sat at them from morning to night, reading newspapers, eating malts or cooing to their steadies. Mothers would split sandwiches with children as uncles and aunts came in for pie and coffee. The counters were streamlined, modern and popular.

Dime stores, called variety stores later, occupied prime corners in most Midwestern towns and customers stocked up on many things they needed. When lunch counter cooks heated up the grills and started frying onions, customers at the far end of the store couldn't resist a quick lunch or snack. The stools filled up fast.

The counters started out being long and straight, but later U-shaped sections were added, which allowed people more elbowroom and a chance to talk more easily. More diners could be seated in a smaller amount of space and the waitress could take their orders quickly.

Closing of the Dime Stores: The End of an Era

In 1997, the Woolworth's company president announced Woolworth's would be closing all of their 400 plus variety stores in the United States and hundreds more abroad. This made people dash to the nearest location and take a final nostalgic look around. Thousands came out on the day of the closings to say goodbye.

Kresges evolved into the K mart Corporation, which had opened its first discount department store in Garden City, Michigan, in 1962. Seventeen additional stores were opened that year, but in 1987, K mart sold the remaining Kresge stores to the McCrory Company.

The closings of the five-and-dime stores in downtown Minneapolis were Kresge's in 1968, where now stands a Greek grill and cluster of lawyer's offices, W.T. Grant's in 1975 and Woolworth's in 1983.

Though Dime Store destiny was entwined with the fate of America's urbanity, its legacy continues in the minds of Baby Boomers who remember the place where everyone had once felt rich.

WISH UPON A STAR WITH
DION AND THE BELMONTS
Buddy Holly Story
STEREO
COLUMBIA
FIRESIDE
SING ALONG WITH MITC
BOBBY VINTON
PAUL ANKA SINGS HIS BIG 15
wand
COLUMBIA
Epic

Chapter 9
MUSIC

My Love for Music

My love for music was kindled as I watched my two older sisters dance in our living-room to 45s played on the record player. Often they were waiting for their boyfriends to arrive in their convertibles. One convertible was yellow and white, the other was pink and white. I envied my sisters in those days. In their pony tails and quilted circle skirts they taught me how to Lindy at age ten.

The songs I remember from those times were "From a Jack to a King" and "Waterloo." The singers were Perry Como, Imogene Coca and Natalie Wood. We watched the Mitch Miller Show every week on TV, and we would sometimes sing along with the bouncing ball. Lawrence Welk and Ed Sullivan too.

Patrol Picnic

In sixth grade it was a great honor to be in school patrol. It was something everyone looked forward to. Only the kids that walked to school could be patrols because you had to go home, eat your lunch quickly and then get back to the patrol post in time to usher the other kids who were coming back to school across the street. Some stops were busier than others. The one on Lowry and Grand was the busiest.

The patrol captains were chosen on a monthly ba-sis and it was always the most popular kids that made it. It didn't seem to matter how responsible you were; it was based strictly on popularity. The patrol captain's job was to go around to every post and make sure everything was running smoothly.

I think we only had about 4 or 5 spots where there was enough traffic to warrant a patrol station. Gary was the heartthrob of our class at the time and he almost always was chosen and got to wear the special leather belt with a big badge across his chest that said Captain. He was kind of conceited about it. Every girl had a crush on Gary including me. One summer day in sixth grade my friend and I spent an hour at the park taking turns kissing Gary on a dare.

At the end of the school year, as a reward for being a patrol, we all got to go to the patrol picnic. This was the highlight of the year. I have sweet memories of that day. Kids came from all over the city for the event. We went to Excelsior Amusement Park, rode on the rides and were treated to a special talent show. That was the best part. A good-looking seventh grader with dark hair sang the song "Runaway." I had never heard the song before. All the girls stood up on the bleachers and screamed their heads off. I think his name was Chuck Schoen and he went on to become part of the well known group The

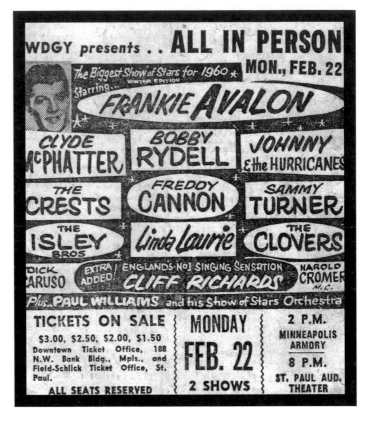

Del Counts. He also went to our high school for a year or two. That was fifty years ago and every time I hear the song "My Little Runaway" I still remember that day.

School Dances

I remember school dances fondly. I went to Northeast Junior High for one year, which only held dances once a month. But then I transferred to Sheridan, where school dances were held every week. I loved those dances. They were held on Friday nights and chaperoned by teachers, who also played the records. The gym was pretty dark except for a small light almost like a silver disco ball in the center. Most of the kids stood along the walls. On occasion, if I close my eyes I can put myself back in time. I'll never forget when the most popular boy in school came over and asked me to dance. Johnny Pachorek was in 9th grade and I was still in seventh. "The Lion Sleeps

Tonight" was playing, and I was wearing my long-sleeved white blouse with ruffles at the cuffs and a soft green plaid jumper. It was the thrill of my lifetime. With the lights down low, we were dancing the standard dance of the time, the Coliseum—sometimes called the Walk. I still wonder to this day why he picked me. I was such a geek and was so shy. Did I look cute or did he just feel sorry for me?

Later I remember dancing to "She Loves You" with Weazer. He was one of the popular boys that I had a crush on for a long time. He had kind of a bad boy image, but was really sweet. I remember our first and only date when he sang "Sweet Genevieve" to me while throwing little stones in the air while we were waiting for the city bus to come. He sure knew how to dance.

They would play records for us in the gym after lunch. We would gulp down our food and hurry over there. Sometimes, if there was a couple dancing in a unique style, the crowd would form a circle around them and watch. One time Weazer and I were in the circle. I got so embarrassed I couldn't dance and left the gym. I remember him later as he walked down the aisle for ninth grade graduation wearing white saddle shoes with his suit. He stuck out like a sore thumb.

It seemed like everyone danced in those days. Girls danced together all the time, we never thought it was a big deal. At home my friends and I practiced dancing the Twist, Fly, Mashed Potatoes, Swim, Wautusi, Coliseum (or the Walk), Lindy, Jerk, Fish, Bird, Egyptian Walk, Chlipso, Locomotion, the Stroll, Barracuda, Freddy.

Junior High

In Junior High, my friends and I hung out at the drugstores near our school. We sat at the counters on bar stools and drank lime, cherry and chocolate cokes. We had school dances every week and also danced in the cafeteria after lunch. On the weekends sometimes we went to the Ritz Theater, which cost twenty-five cents. It didn't matter what was playing, as we went whether we liked the movie or not. We would look around to see who was there. The seats in the back row were used for purposes other than viewing the movie from afar. How I envied those that sat there. I wished I were popular enough to have someone to neck with.

My good friends were Pat Morgan, Jeannie Gentry, Roxanne Fussy, Lee Ann Groen and Nancy Gage. The two memorable events of my ninth grade year were the Beatle's first appearance on the Ed Sullivan show and the assassination of President Kennedy a few months later. Everyone remembers what he or she was doing that fateful day.

The Day John F Kennedy was Shot

On November 22, 1963, I was in ninth grade Algebra class when I first heard the news. Mr. Micolacek was called out of the room and when he returned, he told the class, "President Kennedy has been shot!" It was a terrible shock and there were gasps throughout the room. One of my classmates said, "Good, I voted for Nixon." We gave her the cold shoulder after that for quite awhile. Throughout America people of all ages were glued to their TV sets. Coverage was on every channel. I remember the soldiers from every branch of the service guarding Kennedy's body in the rotunda. Often the station would replay the footage of the actual shooting. A few days later, we watched the slow moving motorcade and procession of the body, pulled by horse and buggy. As we mourned our president, we watched his family mourn for him too. The things I remember most vividly are Jackie with a black veil covering her face and little John-John waving his flag. How terrible it must have been for her to mourn in front of the public.

Journalists compared the similarities of the event

to the assassination of President Lincoln. They were both killed while on their way to, or actually attending, a theater event which they had been warned not to attend. Kennedy's secretary's name was Lincoln and Lincoln's secretary was named Kennedy. And they were both succeeded by a Vice President named Johnson.

It was a shock to our generation that this could happen in a country we once thought was safe. It caused an uneasiness for years to come that someone could be so evil as to kill a president, and this was compounded as we witnessed the point-blank murder of the assassin, Lee Harvey Oswald, by Jack Ruby.

The Beatles on the Ed Sullivan Show

Some say that The Beatles' first appearance on *The Ed Sullivan Show* was the most important event in the history of rock music. Be that as it may, those of us in our fifties remember with fondness the excitement that was created by these four young men from Liverpool.

We remember being mesmerized in front of our small black & white television sets on Sunday, February 9, 1964, at 8 p.m. when the Beatles made their American debut.

The CBS Television office had been overwhelmed with more than 50,000 requests for tickets to a studio that held only 703 seats. The Beatles sang five songs in the following order: "All My Loving," "Till There Was You," "She Loves You," "I Saw You Standing There," and "I Want to Hold Your Hand." Seventy-three million people watched the new group that night. Their appearance had such an impact that most normal activities in America came to a standstill. All eyes were glued to the tube. When the camera focused on John

Lennon as the Beatles sang "Till There Was You," television stations superimposed the words, "Sorry Girls, He's Married." After that performance, mass hysteria erupted wherever the Beatles appeared. Beatlemania had arrived.

In those early days, before they became so eccentric, the Beatles dressed in clean-cut, dark suits and ties. The only thing really unusual about them was their short mop-top hairdos, which were considered outrageous at the time. But boy, could they play music. To this day, my niece reminds me of how I went up to my TV set and kissed George Harrison. Remember I was only fifteen.

Viet Nam 1969

In 1969, the Viet Nam war was on everyone's mind. All across the country college students were staging protests as young adult men were returning home in body bags. I remember a schoolmate of mine who lost his brother. He was never the same after that.

In some ways the war was already winding down

when the government came up with the idea for the lottery. It was a way of letting people know who was likely to be sent overseas and who would be lucky enough to stay home. Those men who had received high numbers could relax and go on with their lives. We all waited anxiously to find out who would go and who would stay.

Before then, my boyfriend was considered a 1A-the prime classification. He had already passed his physical, as in those days almost anyone could. There were rumors about young guys who purposely harmed their bodies to avoid being drafted. Some stood close to loud machinery for days so their ears would become damaged. Others got married, had kids, and went to school to avoid the draft. Some even ran away to Canada.

People gathered around their radios and TV's waiting for the announcement of the draft numbers. All eligible males above the age of eighteen were included. The numbers were drawn according to birth dates. So, each name was drawn from the hat and the dates for the whole year were listed in the order they would be drafted. Men born on the first date drawn would be the first to go.

We were ecstatic when we found out my boyfriend's birthday was picked as number 343. It was very unlikely the draft call would reach that far into the pool before the young men born that following year became eligible. He would not have to go.

The war ended a few years later and the troops came home. My boyfriend never had to go to Viet Nam. Sometimes when I hear the music from the sixties I conjure up that feeling of dread I experienced when everything had been so uncertain. The song Blowin' in the Wind sums it up pretty well. How many roads must a man walk down before they can call him a man? How many deaths will it take till he knows that too many people have died? The answers, my friend, are blowing in the wind. The answers are blowing in the wind.

Popularity of Records

Advances in technology after World War II nurtured rock and roll and the culture that flourished with it. Even on a modest allowance, teenagers could now afford to buy small transistor radios and tune in to their favorite deejay. And the new LP—the 33 rpm long playing record—had much better sound than the old 78s. In fact, the 78s our parents listened to wouldn't play on many of the newer record players.

But it was the 45 rpm record that conquered the teen nation. Small and practically indestructible, the 45 contained as much music as the 78 and had better sound. 45s could be bought for as little as 69 cents a piece in 1957. Teens could stack 10 of these seven inch singles on the spindle of a portable record player and make their own party. More than 70 percent of records were purchased by teenagers in the U.S. in 1958. Most of them were spinning rock and roll music at 45 revolutions per minute [rpm].

We traded 45s and 33⅓ albums. The ultimate was to save up enough money to buy your own record player. Then there were record changers and round inserts for the record player. We had to make sure the needle was kept clean and free from dust. A ball point needle was the best.

I still have my old record player and one of those round record changers too. It's all beat to heck, but I don't have the heart to throw it away. There are so many memories that surround it.

Hit Parade 1950s: From Pop to Rock

Pop stars like Rosemary Clooney, Perry Como, Teresa Brewer, Nat King Cole, Patti Page, and Johnny Mathis were repeat performers in the 1950s Hit Parade. Every week a group of singers including a few guest stars would sing the top ten songs of the week. Hit Parade was broadcasted every Saturday night on NBC at 9:30 to 10:00 PM. The Hit Parade Singers became popular. Well-known stars such as Snooky Lanson, Gogi Grant, Dorothy Collins, June Valli, and Eddy Fisher got their start on the Hit Parade show. Gisele McKenzie was my favorite.

A new generation of clean-cut singers filled the jukeboxes in the '50s, along with perennial favorites like Frank Sinatra and a few Big Bands that lingered on from earli-

Do You Remember These Songs of the '50s?

"If I Knew You Were Comin' I'd a Baked a Cake"— Eileen Barton

"On Top of Old Smoky" — The Weavers

"Come On-a My House" — Rosemary Clooney

"Mockin' Bird Hill" — Patti Page

"Young-at-Heart" — Frank Sinatra

"Sh-Boom" — The Crew-Cuts

"Three Coins in the Fountain" — The Four Aces

"We're Gonna Rock Around the Clock" — Bill Haley and His Comets

"Yellow Rose of Texas" — Mitch Miller

"Ain't That a Shame" —Pat Boone

"Sincerely" —The McGuire Sisters

"Mr. Sandman" — The Chordettes

"Come Softly to Me" — The Fleetwoods

"Don't Be Cruel" — Elvis Presley

"The Great Pretender" — The Platters

"The Wayward Wind" — Gogi Grant

"Whatever Will Be, Will Be" — Doris Day

"Heartbreak Hotel" — Elvis Presley

"Tammy" — Debbie Reynolds

"Love Letters in the Sand" — Pat Boone

"Young Love" — Tab Hunter

"Chances Are" — Johnny Mathis

"Little Darlin'" — The Diamonds

"Bye Bye Love" — The Everly Brothers

er years. Romantic ballads from solo vocalists like Eddie Fisher, Rosemary Clooney, and Kay Starr, as well as close harmony from quartets like the Four Aces, kept couples dancing cheek to cheek. There were also plenty of light hearted novelties like Patti Page's "How Much is that Doggie in the Window?" and kids jitterbugged to Teresa Brewer's "Music! Music! Music!" Rosemary Clooney's "Come On-a My House" was a swinging hit. Clooney recorded 31 top-40 hits from 1951 through 1954. Time magazine put her on its cover, noting that she sounded "the way pretty girls next door ought to sound." Johnnie Ray's renditions of "Cry" and "The Little White Cloud That Cried" got live audiences so fired up they would storm the stage.

Country singer and bandleader Bill Haley rocketed out of obscurity to a spot on the pop chart in 1954 with his version of "Shake, Rattle, and Roll," which rhythm-

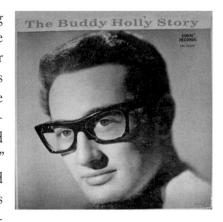

and-blues singer Big Joe Turner had made popular in earlier years. Haley's hit was the first loud rumble of what *Life* magazine called a "frenzied teenage music craze." In 1955 Haley and his group the Comets scored big when featured in Blackboard Jungle, a movie about high-school toughs. When the lights came up, the teenagers in the audience were itching to rock around the clock and the adults were shaking their heads. That same year, singer-songwriter Chuck Berry stepped up the heat with "Maybellene." His next big hit, "Roll Over, Beethoven," released in 1956, announced the rock and roll revolution in no uncertain terms.

Rock and roll had arrived, and with it a new superstar named Elvis Presley made the leap from regional to national stardom in 1956. He released the million-copy singles "Heartbreak Hotel," "Don't Be Cruel" and "Hound Dog." Although the airwaves were soon being inundated by rock and roll, there was room for new stylists like Johnny Mathis, who chose singing over a spot on the 1956 Olympic track team.

Music Culture

Radio continued to be the primary means of listening to music. The major development was a change from primarily AM to FM. Transistor radios became

LAND OF 1000 DANCES

The Twist	Let's Turkey Trot
The Continental Walk	Twistin' Postman
Bossa Nova	Hully Gully
Cool Jerk	Shimmy Like Kate
The Hucklebuck	Baby, Do the Philly Dog
Pony Time	Shimmy Shimmy
The Fly	Monster Mash
Limbo Rock	Funky Broadway
Popeye the Hitchhiker	Do the Clam
The Stroll	Mashed Potato Time
Bristol Stomp	Gravy (For My Mashed Potatoes)
The Jitterbug	
Boogaloo Down Broadway	Do the Bird
Do the Freddie	Pop Pop Pop-Pie
The Mess Around	The Dog
S-W-I-M	Walking the Dog
Do the Monkey	Do the Funky Chicken
The Jerk	Do the Funky Penguin
The Loco-Motion	The Watusi

really popular for teenagers. Radio was supplemented by American Bandstand which was watched by teens from coast to coast. They not only learned the latest music on the program, but how to dance to it. When Chubby Checker introduced the twist on the show in 1961, a new craze was born and dancing became an individual activity. The Mashed Potato, Swim, Watusi, Monkey and Jerk followed the Twist, mimicking their namesakes. Each new dance often lasted for just a song or two before the next one came along. Eventually the names and stylized mimicry ceased and the dancers just moved however they wanted. For those who preferred watching the dancers, Go-go girls danced on stages or in birdcages above the crowd.

Dances

The Stroll

The classic line dance of the 1950's is still danced today to slow swing and rhythm and blues. It is popular throughout the swing scene in Europe, though it's an American dance. Strolling was also part of the film American Graffiti (George Lucas.) The Stroll is done where two parallel lines—boys on one side, girls on the other—faced each other, shifting from left to right, then back again. The fun came when the couple met in the middle to strut down the aisle, all eyes on them. They perform a "shine" routine; at the end, then separate and rejoin the lines. This formation is part of many "contra" dances that were done in the US and Europe for centuries.

The Stroll became recognizable due in large part to American Bandstand that began in 1954. The show's regulars created the popular dance called the Bunny Hop. Following this, they began churning out new dances for every new beat. The dance was inspired by Chuck Willis' hit C.C. Rider. Willis was dubbed "King of the Stroll." The dance soon got a song of its own when Dick Clark suggested to the Diamonds that they create a song specifically for the dance. Famous for their song, "Lil Darlin'" of 1957, they struck gold again with The Stroll. It is well known for its opening line, "Come, let's Stroll."

The Hand Jive

The Hand Jive was a phenomenon in the summer of 1958. It was in the Top Ten for 16 weeks, and remained popular for almost four months.

In 1955, Johnny Otis started his own label, Dig Records, to showcase his own work as well as his latest discoveries. He set the R&B and pop charts ablaze in 1958 with his shave-and-a-haircut beat, Willie and the Hand Jive. During the late '50s, Otis hosted his own variety program on L.A. television, starring his entire troupe and did a guest shot in a 1958 movie, Juke Box Rhythm.

The dance consists of various hand movements-- Slap thighs, cross palms, pound fists together, touch elbows, and extend thumb as if to hitch-hike. It is incredibly easy to learn, since it is repeated without change over six choruses of the song. No wonder everyone in 1958 could do the Hand Jive!

Dance and Stay Young
At The Fabulous

PROM
CENTER

APRIL DANCE SCHEDULE

WED.—OVER 21 NITE
J. HERMAN
Cocktail & Beverage Service
THURS.—OLD TIME MUSIC
SAT.—MODERN MUSIC
2 BANDS
SUN—MODERN MUSIC
JULES HERMAN

Sat., Apr. 1 — AL NOYCE & HIGHLITES
Sun., Apr. 2 — JULES HERMAN
EASTER DANCE
Tue., Apr. 4 — ALL STAR TEEN DANCE
(over)

Music and Local Bands of the Sixties

There was a time when teenagers had their own special dance clubs. They'd pack the place on Friday and Saturday nights and looked forward to it all week.

You paid your admission, got your hand stamped and entered a Teenage Paradise.

Danceland in Excelsior was the largest of local dance halls. Danceland was acquired by Excelsior Park in 1928. In the 1960's it was run by Ray Colihan, know as "Big Reggie" and featured his own dance band. There were times when it would draw up to a thousand teens in one night. That gave way to "stomp" bands like the Trashmen. Legend has it that the kids stomped so hard one night on the floor that it gave way and the kids dropped 11 ft. into the basement, but Big Reggie insisted that the band keep playing. Danceland's license was suspended in 1966 when the Minneapolis gang the "Suprees" started a fight with a baseball bat. It closed for good in 1968 and burned to the ground on July 8, 1973. Excelsior Park closed the weekend after Labor Day 1973 and the carousel was sold to Valleyfair.

The Prom Center in St. Paul lasted the longest. There was a cluster of dance clubs around the intersection of Lake and Nicollet in Minneapolis—Mr. Lucky's, Mr. Magoo's and the New City Opera House. Some of the

Top bands of the era: (Left, from top) Underbeats, Chancellors, Del Counts; (above) Trashmen

other favorite dance clubs were Marigold Ballroom on 13th and Nicollet; Schlief's Little City in West St. Paul; The Purple Barn and Marion Ballroom in Bloomington; and the Bel Rae Ballroom in New Brighton.

Guitar playing teenagers in sharp suits and skinny ties got their start playing at ballrooms, school dances and soda-pop clubs. Garage bands like the Accents and Gregory Dee and the Avanties started cutting records of their own and played the teeny bopper circuit of the Upper Midwest.

Excitement hung in the air as one of these local bands would go on at Danceland. The bands would feed off of the intensity in the room and take requests from the audience. There was no call for original music. Kids just wanted to hear the hits. The Bops play-list included anything that was heard on the radio: the

The High Spirits

Beach Boys, Chuck Berry, Rickie Nelson, Jerry Lee Lewis or Del Shannon.

Dozens of teenagers from high schools all over the Twin Cities came to dance to their favorite local bands. The Underbeats, Chancellors, Del Counts and the High Spirits were local favorites. These local groups sometimes scored a regional hit, for example "Liar Liar," "The Grind" and "Little Latin Lupe Lu." The crowd went crazy over these songs. Very few bands made it big on a national scale, although the Castaways toured with the Beach Boys and opened for Sonny and Cher. The Trashmen, four garage rockers from Robbinsdale, Minnesota, appeared on American Bandstand to play their hit "Surfin Bird."

"Surfin' Bird" was actually a hybrid of two songs made popular by an R&B group called the Revingtons—"Papa-oom-mow-mow" and "Bird's the Word." The Trashmen combined elements of the two along with a smattering of surf talk, and ended up with a double-time piece of mindless and repetitive yammering, with such memorable lyrics as:

Don't you know about the bird?
Well, everybody knows that the bird is a word.
Bird, bird, bird. Bird, bird's a word.

There were very few chords and a lot of beat, and today the song sounds more like an anticipation of The Talking Heads than a 1960s R & B concoction. But when the Trashmen performed the song at Chubb's Ballroom, the crowd went wild, and the song went on to become a nationwide hit. With this, the Trashmen brought the "Minnesota Sound" into national prominence. "Surfin Bird" rose to number four on the Billboard charts early in 1964, only to be unexpectedly knocked down by the Beatles. That year the band itself toured the country playing 289 one-night gigs.

Whatever else they may have been, "Surfin Bird" and other popular songs of the times were innocent and uncomplicated—a way, perhaps, of drowning out the war that had already begun to escalate.

In 1965 the NOVAS debuted their recording, "The Crusher" named after the wrestler Reggie "The Crusher" Lisowski, who performed on All Star Wrestling.

1964 was the breakout year for St. Louis Park musician David Rivkin. He and his brother Bobby associated with three major Twin City bands. The Chancellors had huge local hits with "Little Latin Lupe Lu," and "So

(left top) Joker's Wild, 1967; (left bottom) Wolfman Jack with Musical Theater Co. 1976; (above) Del Counts at Mr. Nibs, 1976

Fine." In 1965 David joined the High Spirits; then later moved to join Stillroven, who recorded, "Hey Joe" and "Little Picture Playhouse." David went on in the music business as a producer and engineer.

1965 saw the High Spirits become major players in the local music scene. The group's first hit was "Turn on your Love Light." "Bright Lights, Big City" was issued in 1967. They received much airplay on Twin Cities' radio.

Band promoters who knew the teen club system well, liked to start out a new band at the Barn, which was literally a barn, or the Marigold Ballroom, or the Prison in Burnsville. If the teens liked the band, the word would spread and the band would get booked for schools and colleges. The teen clubs were a way of promoting the bands. Chuck Schoen of the Del Counts says he never went to his own high school prom, but played for it. From 1965 to 1970, he played for just about every high school event in the city.

In those days it was easier to get air time on the radio than today and bands played for the fun of it. Audiences of teens came ready to dance and Minneapolis became a hot bed for local bands because if the radio disc jockeys liked a band's style of music, they would play it on the air.

TOP SONGS OF THE 1960s

Hey Jude • The Beatles 1968

(I Can't Get No) Satisfaction • The Rolling Stones 1965

Yesterday • The Beatles 1965

I Want To Hold Your Hand • The Beatles 1964

The House Of The Rising Sun • The Animals 1964

The Sounds Of Silence • Simon & Garfunkel 1966

Like a Rolling Stone • Bob Dylan 1965

(Sittin' On) The Dock of the Bay • Otis Redding 1968

Paint It, Black • The Rolling Stones 1966

The Theme from "A Summer Place" • Percy Faith 1960

Downtown • Petula Clark 1965

The Lion Sleeps Tonight • the Tokens 1961

Turn! Turn! Turn! • The Byrds 1965

You've Lost That Loving Feeling • The Righteous Brothers 1965

California Dreamin' • the Mamas and Papas 1966

Can't Buy Me Love • the Beatles 1964

Mrs. Robinson • Simon & Garfunkel 1968

Runaway • Del Shannon 1961

I Heard it through the Grapevine • Marvin Gaye 1968

Leaving on a Jet Plane • Peter, Paul & Mary 1969

Aquarius, Let the Sunshine In • The Fifth Dimension 1969

Mr. Tambourine Man • The Byrds 1965

Ode to Billie Joe • Bobby Gentry 1967

Wild Thing • the Troggs 1966

I Got You Babe • Sonny & Cher 1965

Stop in the Name of Love • the Supremes 1965

Louie, Louie • the Kingsmen 1963

The Locomotion • Little Eva 1962

It's My Party • Leslie Gore 1963

That's how the hits were made, something unheard of in today's music world.

The band didn't even have to be good. Twin Cities Bands like the Bops were booked steadily, headlining for the Rolling Stones when they appeared at Danceland in 1963. To be a legitimate band you needed two things--a publicity picture and a business card. A distinctive "look" was also a plus. The Unbelievable Uglies wore garish plaid pants and other atrocious clothes, for example, though they also signed a record deal with Liberty and opened for the Who.

The most striking contrast between the music scene now and then was that the sixties offered dancing teens a place of their own; now they have primarily sit-down shows. It's harder and more expensive for today's kids to hear a live band. In a way, MTV has made everything easier and less exciting. Dance clubs were a great way to release pent-up energy. The kids just wanted to dance. There were two basic dances--an enfolded slow dance and a fast dance which was a bird-like operation with leg movements that went with the bass. There were very few skilled dancers.

As a rule, the dance clubs were safe, well-run establishments where kids behaved themselves. They never really had serious trouble. Once in a while a fight might break out. Most agree it was a more innocent time. Alcohol did not play a significant role; neither did drugs. By today's standards it was like Little League.

In the late sixties, the Minneapolis Armory promoted the Battle of the Bands nights where kids could pay two bucks and hear ten bands. Music became important and added to a sense of solidarity among the young generation of the sixties. It was a fun time. Some described it as the new Age of Rock.

Transistor Radios

The first radios were made with valve receivers and very expensive. People bought radio kits that they put together themselves to save money. Soon large table-top models were produced, initiating a new form of family entertainment. When the transistor was invented in the early 50's, radios became portable and eventually more affordable: It was the beginning of a new era for radio.

The very first commercially available transistor radio was produced by Regency Electronics. They made the Regency 7R-1 and it was on the shelves for Christmas of 1954. Within a few years, the prices of transistor radios had fallen and the market began to explode. In 1956, Regency Electronics began to offer transistor radios in black, white, red, and gray. Later new shades were introduced and some were offered at a higher price simply because of their unique colors.

Japan jumped into the market in the late 50's and the Sony company began to rake in their share of the sales.

Radios became smaller and smaller and companies used cheaper materials to make them more accessible to everyone while turning a greater profit. Transistor radios could be listened to with headphones and families began to turn away from the tradition of sitting around the radio as each member listened to their own programs on personal radios. Rock and Roll edged radio along even further as young people all needed to be able to listen to the latest songs.

Popular Radio Stations

Minneapolis/St. Paul was typical in the sixties in that there were two fierce top-forty competitors slugging it out. On the west side of the Mississippi, Storz outlet WDGY at 50 kilowatts... and in St. Paul, KDWB, which was 5 kilowatt days, 500 watts night. On KD the jocks were more clever, the music hipper and the format not terribly structured. Some real greats were there, especially in the late 50s through late 60s.

Bill Diehl was probably the best known of the hard-driving WDGY radio disc jockeys. He pitched the songs to a youthful audience in a radio format called "The Top 40." The disc jockeys had a stack of the 40 top records and they played them over and over with the most popular song played at least once every hour. As music director at "Wee Gee," it was Diehl's job to pick the hits. A lot of the big hits started in the Twin Cities. There were songs that might not have gotten played nationwide except that they were playing them in Minneapolis and St. Paul.

N° 831333 B

dial diehl

WDGY

one - one - three - o
SAT. 6 to 7 P. M.
"Top Tune" Time

FREE PRIZES — Many valuable prizes given away every week. Nothing to buy. Listen to the Hi-Fi Club on WDGY every week. Your number may be drawn during the broadcast.
Sponsored by
Coca-Cola Bottling Company
Minneapolis - St. Paul

HAL MURRAY
6:00 - 10:00 A.M.

ART WAY
10:00 - 2:00 P.M.

JIM O'NEILL
2:00 - 6:00 P.M.

LOU RIEGERT
6:00 - 9:00 P.M.

RANDY COOK
9:00 - 12:00 P.M.

DON DUCHENE
Midnight - 6:00 A.M.

BOB SALMON
6:00 - 12:00 P.M.
Saturday
6:00 - 11:00 P.M.
Sunday

D. J. LEARY
"Hotline"
11:05 - 12:00 P.M.
Sundays

KDWB | FABULOUS FORTY SURVEY

FOR WEEK ENDING MARCH 23, 1963

This Week			Last Week
1. *Rhythm Of The Rain	The Cascades—Valiant		1
2. The End Of The World	Skeeter Davis—RCA		13
3. *Can't Get Used To Losing You			
	Andy Williams—Columbia		14
4. *Ruby Baby	Dion—Columbia		4
5. Walk Like A Man	The Four Seasons—Vee Jay		2
6. From A Jack To A King	Ned Miller—Fabor		5
7. You've Really Got A Hold On Me			
	The Miracles—Tamla		3
8. *You're The Reason I'm Living	Bobby Darin—Capitol		7
9. *Walk Right In	The Rooftop Singers—Vanguard		6
10. *Don't Say Nothing Bad	Cookies—Dimension		10
11. *Boss Guitar	Duane Eddy—RCA		9
12. *One Broken Heart For Sale /They Remind Me			
Too Much Of You	Elvis Presley—RCA		12
13. *What Will Mary Say?	Johnny Mathis—Columbia		11
14. *In Dreams	Roy Orbison—Monument		16
15. He's So Fine	The Chiffons—Laurie		17
16. *Greenback Dollar	Kingston Trio—Capitol		8
17. South Street	The Orlons—Cameo		19
18. *Pipeline	Chantay's—Dot		21
19. Call On Me	Bobby Bland—Duke		23
20. *Butterfly Baby	Bobby Rydell—Cameo		26

This Week			Last Week
21. *Shut Down	Beach Boys—Capitol		Debut
22. *Let's Limbo Some More /Twenty Miles			
	Chubby Checker—Parkway		25
23. *Mama Didn't Lie	Jan Bradley—Chess		18
24. *Blame It On The Bossa Nova			
	Eydie Gorme—Columbia		24
25. *I Wanna Be Your Lover	Diane Emond—Redcoat		15
26. *Eternally	The Chantels—Ludix		22
27. *Love For Sale	Arthur Lyman Group—Hi Fi		36
28. Sun Arise	Rolf Harris—Epic		28
29. *Hey Paula	Paul and Paula—Phillips		20
30. *Don't Set Me Free	Ray Charles—ABC Paramount		29
31. *Our Day Will Come	Ruby & Romantics—Kapp		39
32. *Zing Went The Strings Of My Heart			
	The Furys—Mack IV		33
33. *Alice In Wonderland	Neil Sedaka—RCA		27
34. *Let's Turkey Trot	Little Eva—Dimension		30
35. *Puff	Peter, Paul & Mary—Warner Bros.		Debut
36. *Amy	Paul Peterson—Colpix		37
37. *Our Songs Of Love	The Love Notes—Wilshire		38
38. *Sandy	Dion—Laurie		40
39. I Will Follow Him	Little Peggy March—RCA		Debut
40. Mr. Bass Man	Johnny Cymbal—Kapp		Debut

*Records First Heard On KDWB

FAVORITE ALBUMS

1. SONGS I SING ON THE JACKIE GLEASON SHOW   Frank Fontain
2. MOVING   Peter, Paul & Mary
3. YOU'RE THE REASON I'M LIVING, Bobby Darin
4. ALL ALONE AM I   Brenda Lee
5. WEST SIDE STORY   Soundtrack

This survey is compiled each week by radio station KDWB, St. Paul, Minnesota. It is a true, accurate and unbiased account of record popularity, based upon sales reports, distributor accounts and all information available to the music staff of KDWB.

Chapter 10

FREEBIES AND FADS

The popularity of stamps, coupons and give-aways was huge in the '50s and '60s. Banks like Twin City Federal gave away place settings of dinnerware or stadium blankets and thermoses for each $25.00 deposited into a savings account. Movie theaters in the 50s gave away Depression glass as incentive to frequent their establishments. You could even pay insurance premiums by saving up Green Stamps and other promotional products. Almost every store was giving away something to entice the shopper to buy their products.

Price wars between gas stations were keen. Sometimes the price was lower at one but the other had the best give aways. My boyfriend and I stopped at the Spur station every time we went to Crystal because they gave away green glasses in different sizes--one free with each fill of gas. I got a whole set of small and large beverage glasses and juice glasses for my Hope Chest. My mother saved blue glasses that came free in Duz detergent.

Saving for my Hope Chest

When I entered high school and was working part time at the Donaldson's lunch counter in downtown Minneapolis, one of my first purchases was a cedar chest. The new cedar chest ended up in my family's living room as storage for extra blankets. Every once in a while, I would glance at it and dream of the man I would marry.

It was every girl's dream to fill a hope chest with practical and treasured items. This was a traditional method for a family to share in the vision of their daughter's future wedded happiness and help her prepare for that time. This was partially where the term "hope chest" originated. They were first called wedding chests, but people later called them hope chests as they "hoped for marriage." Hope chests were traditionally used to store hand embroidered linens and protect them until the bride was ready to use them in her new home. Mine was filled with Tupperware and free glasses and towels that I'd gotten from laundry detergent giveaways and gas station perks.

Some of my wedding gifts came from Green Stamps. We received stacking tables and a decorative balancing scale. Later we purchased two Avocado green lamps for our living room. Perhaps the most fun of it was to go paging through the catalog and dream about the possibilities of what we might choose. Many guests gave out filled green stamp booklets as wedding gifts. The redemption center was at 1108 West Broadway and 1102 Nicollet Avenue during 1958-60 and later at 2111 East Lake Street in Minneapolis.

I remember one day I noticed that my favorite green lamp had a huge crack in it. My two boys and my husband were afraid that I would find out about their secret game of catch one day in the living room, during which one of them had knocked the lamp over. All I could say was, "Thank God, I hated that lamp." I was glad because I could finally buy a new one.

You could get a toaster, which normally cost $4.75, for between 4 and 6¾ books in 1974. I don't think you could return things.

FREEBIES

Green Stamps

Most Baby Boomers fondly remember S & H Green Stamps. The Brady Bunch fought over them on one episode of their show. The stamps became so popular that during the 1960s that three times as many were printed as U. S. postage stamps, and the catolog describing the rewards, bonuses, and merchandise available was the most popular publication in the country.

Retail organizations bought stamps from Sperry and Hutchinson and gave them out as bonuses with every purchase. The more you spent, the more stamps you received. Once you'd saved up a sizable quantity of stamps and pasted them into the books, you could go down to the redemption center (with a sore tongue that tasted like glue) and trade them in for merchandise. The stores footed the bill for the stamps, but felt it was worthwhile because it fostered customer loyalty. Customers flocked to the stores that gave out Green Stamps, even if their prices were slightly higher (to offset the cost of the stamps), because they loved the accumulation of "free" wealth that the rising mound of completed stamp books represented, and also the

"free" merchandise you could get with them, which ranged from toasters to silver tea sets. One school in Erie, Pennsylvania saved up 5.4 million Green stamps to buy a pair of gorillas for a local zoo! Stamp companies created different colored stamps, which included Orange, Yellow, K&S Red, Pinky, Gold Bond, Blue Chip, and Plaid. Other stamps were Top Value, Mor-Valu, Shur-Valu, Big Bonus, Double Thrift, Buckeye, Buccaneer, Two Guys, King Korn, Eagle and Regal. Green Stamps were probably the most popular of the competing stamp companies.

The stamp program faded away during the recession of the 1970s, as stores began to advertise "Everyday Low Prices" rather than complicated merchandise schemes. With the birth of the Internet, however, green Stamps made a remarkable rebound, and today, if you have boxes of Green Stamps still tucked away in your attic, there's good news; you can still redeem them for cash or merchandise at Greenpoints.com.

Gold Bond Stamps

Curt Carlson founded Gold Bond in 1938 on $55 of borrowed capital. Noting with interest the relatively new practice of giving out trading stamps as a premium to customers, he saw that it built customer loyalty. The original company was a mail drop slot and desk in the Plymouth Building in downtown Minneapolis. Years of struggle eventually led to his landing a major client—the Super Valu Food Store chain. Both locally and around the country, customers received an allotment of Gold Bond Stamps with their purchases. Many people today can remember when their moms sat them down at the kitchen table to glue stamps into books. Trading stamps became extremely successful. The redemption center for Gold Bond was on Highway 100 and 55.

Arleen Carlson helped her husband establish his company. Noted for her bright smile and soft voice, she dressed in a majorette's costume to promote the introduction of stamps into local stores. Her loving style became her personal hallmark. Even in later years, when she had become confined to a wheelchair, she insisted on attending company and civic functions to demonstrate her support. By the late 1960s, when companies began losing interest in trading stamps, Curt Carlson transformed his Gold Bond Stamp business into the Carlson Companies.

Free Glassware and Towels

On Saturday afternoons in the 60s there was a line up of TV country music shows that concluded with Hee Haw at 6 p.m. A Country and Western music review

Memories of S & H Green Stamps
Pam Albinson

When I was eleven years old, it was a big deal to redeem our S and H Green Stamps. It was like getting a special gift. I remember going to the grocery store and waiting for the stamps to come out of the machine next to the cash register. It made the sound of--tick, tick, tick--as they came out in sheets. One for every dollar you spent. When we got home we'd put them inside a special drawer. It was like a Christmas drawer to us; something to dream about. We could hardly wait to get enough stamps to cash in. Every so often, my Mom and I would spend the night pasting stamps into our little books. Sometimes the pages rippled and the book would be so thick we'd have to put a rubber band around it. There were 50 stamps on a page and twenty-four pages in a book.

No one had much money in those days so we'd brag about the items we got by redeeming our Green Stamps. The things I remember getting were a funky rod iron lamp and metal canister set. It was so much fun to talk about what we might get. We'd page through the book with wide eyes and trembling fingers. Sometimes we would exchange our Gold Bond Stamps with friends for their Green Stamps. It seemed sneaky, like we were getting something for nothing. A bonus.

called the Porter Wagoner Show featured Porter and his singing sidekick Dolly Parton. She was just a Tennessee mountain girl then with a beautiful voice. They did duets together and both had bouffant hairdos. It was said that they made a point of dying their hair the same shade of platinum blonde.

Dolly did the Fab detergent commercials, which had a free washcloth in every box of laundry soap. She'd open a package, unfurl a towel and then exclaim, "Looky here, Porter! You can only get 'em in boxes of Fab." It was a plush Cannon towel that came in stripes or solids. Each week Dolly performed a spotlight solo, such as "Coat of Many Colors," which depicted her growing up as a poor country girl and wearing a coat made of rags that her mother had stitched together for her out of scraps. The song was sentimental, and later became a hit.

There was another detergent that had a free glass tumbler inside—Duz. It was a good quality glass that came in different colors. That was how many people got their glassware. There were also towels in boxes of Breeze and Gain.

Duz offered Golden Wheat glasses with matching dishes. The offer for dishes ran from 1963-1966 and the glasses are still being offered today. The 1963 glasses and dishes were trimmed in 22-carat gold. The pattern was described as fronds of wheat which symbolized life, plenty, and the goodwill of men. The glass or dish came directly in the box of Duz detergent. If a glass or dish was broken when you got it, Proctor & Gamble would send you a new one within the month.

In 1965 Duz began to offer Swedish Modern Design glasses, which came in four sizes—juice glasses, goblets, tall iced tea glasses and sculptured tumblers. In 1968, Duz offered Royal Family dishes. This set consisted of a dinner platter offered inside their King-sized boxes that were distinctly marked. Two saucers came in other plainly-marked King sized boxes. A cup was in every Giant size box. In addition to this, Duz would mail either three matching soup bowls or salad plates to you for only $1.50 with an enclosed box top from any size Duz.

Duz offered an American Concord glass in each box of Duz in 1976. The glasses came in four sizes and were smoke-colored with a floral design. In the mid-seventies, one could also purchase a box of Duz that had an American Concord Glass inside and send away for an American Concord Dip 'n Snack Set, which consisted of a matching smoke colored glass bowl and tray.

Betty Crocker Coupons

Remember when collecting a few box tops could get you new silverware or a toaster for your cousin's wedding gift? For more than forty years, General Mills helped stock America's kitchens with affordable, quality merchandise through the Betty Crocker catalog. It was a tradition that touched many generations.

The General Mills Company offered Betty Crocker Points. Packages of Gold Medal Flour, Betty Crocker brownie mix, Cheerios and other products came with clip-and-save coupons on the back that had differing point values. Since the 1930s, millions of customers have swapped these points for discounts on a growing array of rewards such as Oneida stainless flatware, kitchen linens, baking pans that transformed cakes into cathedrals, salad spinners, stockpots and a rainbow of Fiesta dinnerware.

The points program began in 1932 with a coupon tucked inside every sack of Gold Medal Flour and Wheaties cereal box. Consumers who mailed in these coupons would receive a free silver-plated teaspoon. The response was so great that General Mills began to offer an entire set of flatware; its pattern was "Friendship" later renamed "Medality." In 1937, the coupons were printed on the outside of the package.

Those who grew up in the country, and didn't have a lot of access to stores found the cookbooks, gadgets, cookie cutters and knickknacks in the Betty Crocker catalog uniformly enticing. Loyal customers clipped and saved coupons and looked forward eagerly to the arrival of the next catalog, which would contain the newest items on the market.

Family members saved coupons for each other. Young brides saved coupons and collected silverware to put into their hope chests. It was fun to dream about having an entire set of Oneida silverware. Early patterns were Twin Star, Chatelaine, Fire Song, Queen Bess and Beethoven. The catalog helped women outfit their kitchens. Friends and family members always bought things that had coupons so they could help out the bride-to-be.

At its height, in the 1940s through the 1960s, General Mills mailed six to eight Betty Crocker catalogs per year to millions of households across the country. It wasn't unusual to hear of a mom that gave everyone in her family silverware for wedding presents from a cata-

log or a group of ladies who helped refurbish a church kitchen with products from these points.

Later, flyers were added to offer a wider selection of merchandise, and in 1962 the first full catalog was printed. In 1990, the coupons on the packages were re-designed and valued with a new designation of points. In 1997, the online version of the catalog was born and mailings began to dwindle.

The folks at General Mills decided the Fall 2006 catalog would be its last. Sad is the ending of this tradition that's been part of the American culture for decades.

Depression Glass

The term Depression Glass referred to an American-made transparent glassware that was manufactured from the early- to mid-1920s through the end of World War II. Clear crystal glassware made during that same time period was also considered Depression Glass. Some patterns were produced into the 1950s or later.

Many patterns of Depression Glass were distributed as promotional items during the lean years. Depression Glass items would appear in soap or cereal boxes and were given away at local movie theaters or gas stations to encourage patronage. One glass manufacturer was saved from bankruptcy during the Depression when he received an order from Quaker Oats to make five railroad cars full of glass!

There were well over 100 companies manufacturing glass in the United States before the Great Depression, but by the time it ended, less than half remained. Fire was a major cause for a company to cease operations. Factories that burned down during the Depression years were rarely rebuilt. Instead, they would simply go out of business.

The predominant colors for glassware of that era were amber, yellow, pink, green, blue and crystal. Short-run colors were lavender and bright orange. The dominant colors for decorating the home during that era were yellow and amber. Larger quantities of these colors were produced in the beginning, but the demand of later markets seemed to be centered on pink, green, and blue. These colors are priced higher in antique stores today because they are a lot harder to find.

Quite often pieces were priced by the dozen or even by the barrel, which contained five or six dozen glass dishes. Prices of 14 cents each or $1.72 per dozen were common. Vases were sold in groups of six and retailed for less than a dollar a piece. Today these pieces may command hundreds of dollars a piece!

Setting prices for items made more than seventy years ago largely depends upon the demand by collectors and the supply, meaning its availability. Parts of the Midwest are hot spots for Depression glass. Mayfair, Rose of Sharon and Cherry Blossom are popular pink patterns. The green Love Birds pattern is unique and beautiful.

How Cracker Jack Began

Cracker Jack began in 1871, when a German immigrant named Frederick William Rueckheim, who had saved up $200 working on a farm, started selling popcorn made by hand to workers who were rebuilding after the Great Chicago Fire. Later he partnered with his brother Louis to buy some candy-making equipment. The brothers combined peanuts, popcorn, and molasses together and sold their sticky concoction at the Chicago's Columbian Exposition in 1893. People loved the taste, but not the texture.

Eventually Louis made a formula that was still molasses-coated, but dry and crispy. (The formula remains secret to this day.) When a sales person was given a sample he shouted, "That's a crackerjack!" which was slang for something really good. Soon, the brothers copyrighted the name. Cracker Jack was sold in large tubs until a triple-sealed moisture-proof box made of wax was developed to keep its freshness. The popular song "Take Me Out to the Ball Game" (1908) immortalized the product with the line, "Buy me some peanuts and Cracker Jacks," and Cracker Jack became a staple at all big league ballparks in America.

In 1910, the company put coupons in their boxes that could be sent back by mail to redeem prizes. The brothers then had an idea of putting the prize directly into each box, thus eliminating the wait and also the costs of shipping. During World War I, Cracker Jack decorated their box with red, white, and blue stripes. The Sailor Jack logo came from Frederick's grandson and dog that modeled for the company. Shortly after he appeared on the box, Frederick's grandson died.

When the first radio ads aired for Cracker Jack the prizes were plastic and all were wrapped in plastic wrap. Space-age toys during the 50s were a big hit. In 1956 the price was raised from 5 cents to 10 cents a box. High-speed packaging was installed in 1960, and during the 1980s plastic in boxes came to an end. Frito-Lay bought Cracker Jack in 1997, and that same year a nostalgic TV ad for Cracker jack aired at the Super Bowl.

Today's prizes have to meet with safety guidelines so a young child won't get hurt. Some of the guidelines include no sharp objects or things that can be swallowed, and the toy must appeal equally to boys and girls.

Northern Girls

Many women remember framed prints of the American Beauties hanging in their room as a child. Funny, how a product as ordinary as toilet paper can send your mind reeling back through time. You had to send away for these pictures and they were either free with proof of purchase from Northern toilet paper packages or reasonably priced. These young girls came in

white, blue, yellow and green outfits. And, the baby print was of the Northern infant in pink.

Pink—a pretty little baby. Northern tissue is made with fluff, nothing else is soft enough.

Blue—Soft as a blanket, soft as me, that's how soft softness can be. Softness more that I can speak, my kitty snuggled to my cheek.

White—A furry mitten white as snow is not the softest thing I know. Northern tissue is made with fluff nothing else is soft enough.

Green—What is softness? Children know softness is where blossoms grow.

In 1958, Frances Hook's American Beauties appeared in Northern Tissue advertisements and on March 23, 1959 the first rolls featuring them were shipped from the mill. The brand's first "Northern Girls" sent tissue sales rocketing. Offers for prints and the Northern Paper Towel's All American Boys broke records with 30 million sales by 1966. In 1974, Northern Tissue's famous "Northern Girls" made their return on four-packs.

Fads

Day of the Week Panties

"Day of the Week" underpants were a craze in the 1950s. Novelty Day of the Week panties were packaged in fancy gift boxes! The box included seven pairs of underwear with a heart shaped appliqué and the day of the week embroidered on each left front hip. Each pair had a different pastel color starting with Sunday, which was white, then light blue, pink, yellow, lavender, mint green and black, which was for Saturday! The colors each had significance. Black was considered risqué in those days. The box was covered with blue shimmery fabric on all sides and had a unique Pin Up Girl reclining on the front. She was in the style of Big Eye art from the 1960s, wearing a blue body suit and hat with feather. The lid opened by a little fabric tab and was sold also in a pink gift box set.

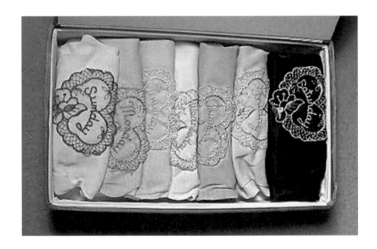

Princess Phone

"...It's Little. It's Lovely. It Lights!" was the marketing slogan of one of the most popular telephones.

Compactness, attractive styling and illuminated dial all contributed to the usefulness of the Princess telephone, which came in white, beige, pink, yellow, blue or turquoise. It lit up when you lifted the handset, and you could keep it on your stand as a nightlight. This Western Electric Princess Phone was the talk of the town—a favorite of teenage girls in the 1960s. Long nights were spent on it talking to a boyfriend or chatting with the girls. Many teens wanted a pink Princess phone to match their gray and pink bedrooms and chenille tufted bedspread. Privacy meant getting out of the living room, where the heavy black phone sat, and where the rest of the family often sat, trying to listen to what you were saying. At least, it seemed that way.

A Princess phone was made of light, new miracle plastic whose lighthearted colors were a sign of coming into womanhood. Sandra Dee had a Princess telephone so that she could talk to Troy Donahue in their popular movies.

You can probably remember one in your sister's room or at your mother's desk. The Princess phone was introduced when an original desk phone was redesigned with a smart new look. The unit had a smaller footprint that fit into those not-so-big spaces, and with its rounded edges, sleek lines and fashionable styling, it quickly became a favorite.

The roots of the Princess phone date back to 1955, when Bell's Merchandising Department wanted to give customers what they asked for. The world was changing, conveniences were becoming commonplace, and people wanted more than just the main phone in the hallway. They wanted a phone that could fit on a bedside table, which would also keep their teenagers out of the main hall! In 1956, the first model of the phone was introduced. A night-light inside was to aid if someone wanted to dial out in the middle of the night. The rotary dial was present on the original model, followed by a ten-button touchtone and then the twelve button touch-tone pad. Rumor has it that these phones were last produced in 1994. It's been said that the public is still leasing some of the original Princesses, and you can still purchase one on-line.

Evening in Paris Perfume

In 1929, Bourgeois of France launched their Evening in Paris perfume label in the United States. Even during the Great Depression this romantic new fragrance was placed in the five and dime stores for 25 cents a bottle and in upscale department stores, packaged in expensive bottles with dazzling crystal stoppers, for considerably more. With this strategy women in all walks of life could pamper themselves and dream of Parisian nights.

It was every girl's wish to have a bottle of Evening in Paris perfume in the 40s and 50s. A blend of floral fragrances, it quickly became a timeless classic. Advertisements said, "…it captures the very soul of Paris and

warms the heart like a romantic evening stroll along the Seine River." By 1955, it had become the Most Famous Fragrance in the World, and its cobalt blue bottle with tall silver cap remained on many women's dressing tables for decades. The boxed set included perfume, cologne and dusting powder, all placed in rich folds of silvery satin.

Yet by the mid-sixties, Evening in Paris had lost its appeal. How a single perfume had held so much influence was truly amazing, and even today there are women who love to reminisce about the blue bottled perfume they had once thought was so glamorous, seductive and inexpensively elegant. You can still find it on EBay and some select vendors like the Vermont Country Store, who are banking on its nostalgic appeal.

Pop-It Beads

These beads came in many shapes, sizes and colors. "Oh, what Fun!" You could use your creativity to make cool bracelets and necklaces. Multicolor, clear, pastels, and pearlescent were probably the most common colors. You could mix and match them or take them apart.

You could make long chain necklaces or double-stranded bracelets. There was something incredible about making

Photos:
New Year's Eve Slumber Party,
1955, Betty Kieley and
Geri Peterson.
Upper right image:
7-Up advertisement, 1954

jewelry to match your outfits. They made a popping sound when you put them together and hurt your foot when you stepped on one.

Pajama Parties

Remember séances and Ouija boards? Bra-freezing and plastic wrap stretched invisibly under toilet seats? A sleepover was the time-honored bonding experience for teenage girls who gathered at a friend's house for an overnight stay. Also called a slumber party, the participants typically stayed up late, talked, listened to music, and played games until they fell asleep. Guests would bring their own pillows and usually other favorite bedtime paraphernalia. It was a luxury to sleep in a sleeping bag during a sleepover. Board games were played, pillow fights were fought, movies were watched, and make-shift forts were constructed out of blankets. Teenagers played records and games like Twister, or spent the night placing prank phone calls.

The more unusual the theme of a slumber party, the more fun it was. A taffy pull, beatnik party, scavenger hunt or scrapbook theme all made for successful slumber parties. There was a great deal of focus on what clothing was worn. Pastel-colored pajamas trimmed in white and huge fuzzy slippers were in style. Quilted, chenille or furry robes trimmed in lace were popular. Polka dot flannel two-piece pajamas and nighties in dotted Swiss, nylon tricot or cotton baby dolls were trendy. Frills and lacey pastels were all the rage.

Pajama parties were idealized in the movies of the 1950s and 60s such as *Pajama Party*, a well-loved sequel

to the vastly popular *Beach Party*, in which Annette Funicello moves indoors for another wonderful romp with the gang. Its tag line was "The Party Picture that takes off where the others pooped out!"

At pajama parties everyone danced in their pajamas, of course.

Lane Cedar Chests

The Lane Company, maker of the iconic Lane Cedar Chest, was located in Alta Vista, Virginia. Edward Hudson Lane founded the company in 1912 at a junction of the Virginian and Southern railways, which allowed for easy transportation of materials and finished products to and from the factory. The company started by making ammunition boxes from pine for the federal government in World War 1.

To meet wartime demands, Lane introduced an efficient assembly system at his factory. When the plant converted to its peacetime production of cedar chests, they adopted some of the mass-production techniques he had learned during the war emergency, which brought him

A Gift from the Orient
Joannie Moses

My grandmother placed her cedar-lined Lane hope chest at the foot of her bed as a young woman and it stayed there until I was ten years old when she passed away in 1955. In it resided her wedding gown, gloves, and silk stockings along with fancy hand-worked towels, baby keepsakes, family photos and other memorabilia.

I cherished the times we went through these precious items together, and enjoyed anchoring the chest in my life by sitting on it whenever Grandma and I spent time in her bedroom. My father knew how much I admired Grandma's chest and the special place it provided for personal treasures.

While my father traveled the Orient on a business trip, he called Mother from Japan in April of 1961 and said, "Watch for a shipment. I just had something very special handmade for Joan and it should arrive in a few weeks."

Within a short time it arrived. My brother and I opened the heavy crate in the garage by prying off slabs of lumber with a crow bar. Finally, perched on the bottom pallet of wood, we uncovered a beautiful black-lacquered hope chest.

Figures made of painted bone, mother of pearl, and ivory depicted the wedding story on the sides and the top of the chest. As I unlatched the scrolled brass fastener and opened the lid, a strong scent of lemon wafted up to me. The lovely chest was lined with lemon wood! It was laden with silk scarves, lengths of cashmere, a German-made HO gauge engine for my brother, and ebony-handled brass flatware from Thailand, yards of exquisitely embroidered satins from Hong Kong and dolls from Japan.

We emptied the decorative chest of its Oriental contents, and I began to fill it with treasures for my future life as a married woman. In the bottom I gently placed my grandmother's wedding dress and other cherished heirloom items.

There was plenty of space left for shower gifts of china, crystal, silver, honeymoon negligees, embroidered kitchen towels and fancy pillowcases. This beautiful hope chest has rested at the foot of my bed and held special memories delicately but securely for the last forty-seven years.

success. Reaching new heights of production and prosperity in the 1920s, Lane began to advertise his products nationally. These advertisements sought to equate the ideal of domesticity with a Lane Hope Chest by showing a young woman storing her clothing or home furnishings inside a beautifully carved wooden chest in anticipation of her marriage was a good idea. This was summed up in the company's tag line, "The gift that starts the home."

Lane advertisements reached a high point during World War II as it persuaded thousands of GI's leaving for overseas to purchase a Lane Hope Chest for the sweethearts they were leaving behind. Ads consisted of images of men in uniforms with their fiancées on their arms accompanied by patriotic slogans and the face of Shirley Temple, who symbolized all things American.

In 1987, Interco Corporation purchased the Lane Company in a hostile takeover and filed for bancruptcy five years later. The last Lane Cedar chest to be manufactured in the United States rolled off the production line in the summer of 2001.

Slam books

Slam books looked like small autograph books or notebooks. Students would pass them around in school all the time. When you received a book, you would add a mean comment about someone you disliked then read the other comments until the teacher took the book from you.

Slam Books were popular during the 60s in junior high. We didn't glue tacks to a teacher's chair, but we'd pass around one of these handmade questionnaires while keeping an eye on the teacher and preparing to quietly close the book if he or she should turn around and see us and snatch the book away. Then everyone would snicker and laugh.

Each page was numbered with a question. If you had number one, then you would fill out the first line of every page. Starting with your name and after that, you would look at who had signed the book so far and read what everyone else had written.

1. Age and Zodiac sign?
2. What are your hobbies?
3. What's your favorite item of clothing?
4. Do you like to swap items like Friendship books, Slams, Decos?
5. Favorite recent movie or movies?
6. Worst recent movie or movies?
7. Best looking actor or actress?
8. Favorite author or teacher?
9. First thing you would buy, if you won a million $$$?
10. What were you doing ½ hour ago?
11. Last record that you bought? Was it any good?

Catalogs

For a one-car family, shopping wasn't easy, and some families didn't have a car at all. The catalogs that arrived in the mail were especially welcome at these households, because women could shop without leaving the house, or simply page through the catalog daydreaming of future purchases. The excitement of receiving the latest catalog was similar in those days to the anticipation

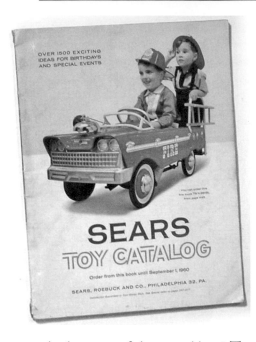

of an upcoming Christmas holiday.

Some of the catalogs were Sears and Roebuck, JC Penneys, Montgomery Wards, Aldens, and Spiegel.

Cereal Box Prize

How many of you can remember when you were a kid and looked forward to the prize in the bottom of the cereal box? There was a certain cereal that promoted Flash Gordon, who was an invincible (but make-believe) superhero. The adventures of Flash Gordon and his companions Dr. Hans Zarkov and Dale Arden featured a journey to the planet Mongo, where the three of them performed good deeds. We bought the cereal mainly to get the prize that came with it. The prize was a Flash Gordon Super Vision shield.

To get to the prize you had to pour the entire box of cereal out because it was at the bottom. Eating the cereal first would have been a good idea but most of us were too impatient to wait. Putting on the shield made you feel like you were invincible, just like Flash Gordon.

In those days, other promotional items in cereal boxes included spoons, bowls and toys like a Buck Rogers Magic Saturn Code Ring. Plastic soldiers that would float when filled with baking soda were also popular. Sometimes the prize was a little disappointing, but we would never admit it.

The cereal boxes themselves had contests, games and masks on the back that also fascinated us. Saving up box-tops to send away for a toy was a popular thing to do too.

Autograph Albums

Rummaging through my box of memories, I came across my autograph album from junior high. A memory of sock hops, slumber parties, rides on the bus to baseball games, going to the Fair and BOYS (remember all those girlhood crushes?) flashed before me as I read through verses written by my schoolmates, relatives and teachers. My relationships with these people have faded, but rereading the verses brought back a rush of sentimental feelings like it was yesterday.

Autograph albums made the rounds at parties and in school. The verses written in them were a hodgepodge of sentiments; some mocking, some complimentary, others wishing you the best, and some that were insulting. Mostly boys wrote these. Many of the verses related to love and marriage. In addition, sayings and symbols were scrawled in the corners and along the sides of the pages, or even upside down.

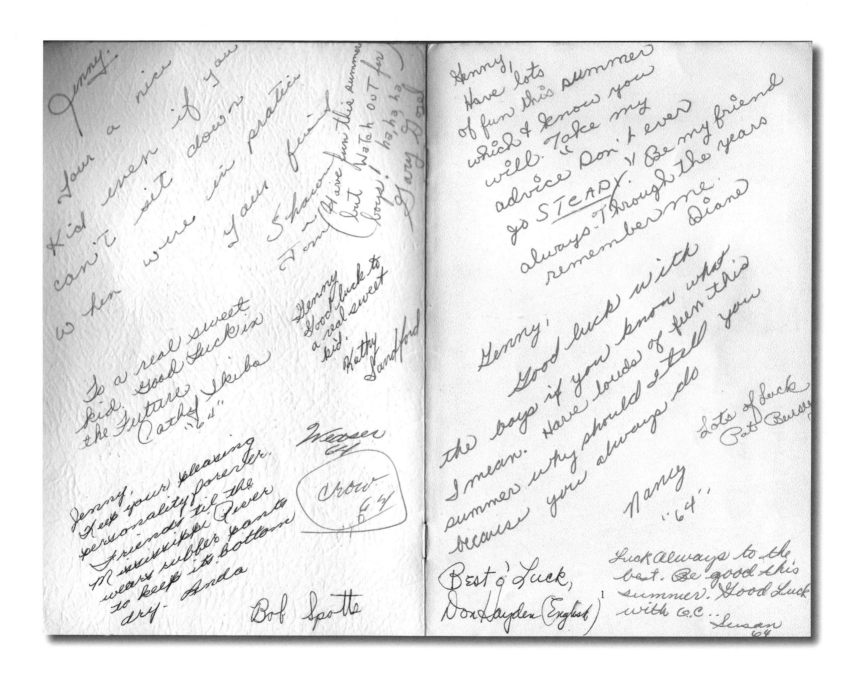

Jenny:
Your a nice
Kid even if you
can't sit down
when were in pratice
Your friend
Tom

To a real sweet
kid, Good Luck in
the Future Skiba
Cathy
"64"

I have fun this summer
but watch out for
boys! hahaha
Gary Dodd

Jenny,
Good luck to
a real sweet
kid.
Kathy
Sandford

Jenny, your pleasing
Keep your
personality forever.
friends 'til the
Mississippi River
wears rubber pants
to keep it's bottom
dry. Anda

Weaser
64

Crow
63

Bob Spotts

Jenny,
Have lots
of fun this summer
which I know you
will. Take my
advice Don't ever
go STEADY. Be my friend
always. Through the years
remember me.
Diane

Jenny,
Good luck with
the boys if you know what
I mean. Have loads of fun this
summer why should I tell you
because you always do
Nancy
"64"

Lots of Luck
Pat Busse

Best o' Luck,
Don Hayden (English) [1]

Luck always to the
best. Be good this
summer. Good Luck
with G.C..
Susan
64

Chapter 11
ATTICS, PANTRIES AND TRADITIONS

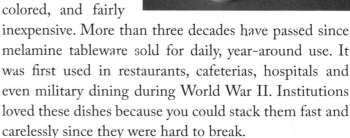

One day I walked into an antique store. In the entry I saw four place settings of Melmac dishes displayed on a small enamel table. They were bright yellow, orange and turquoise. A stack of dinner plates, bowls and cups with saucers. I stared at those dishes for a long time. Then, I picked them up and handled them with care, though, there was no need—Melmac was unbreakable! I wanted so much to buy them that day, but knew I would never use them and they would simply take up space in my house that was already cluttered with old things. What was it about those dishes that still intrigued me so much?

I guess I simply love dishes from the past. The sight of them can take me back to the early sixties when I was growing up in my small neighborhood in Northeast Minneapolis, or to my teenage years, when I stuffed Melmac dishes into my hope chest and dreamed of the day I would get married. Yet there was a time when I didn't think much of those old cheap dishes in our pantry. How interesting it is that sometimes we later cherish the things we once disdained.

Melmac Dishes

The newly-invented plastic dinnerware soon became so popular that by the late 1950s nearly 50 percent of all dishes were molded using melamine. Dishes made of melamine went by the trade name of Melmac. They were durable, brightly colored, and fairly inexpensive. More than three decades have passed since melamine tableware sold for daily, year-around use. It was first used in restaurants, cafeterias, hospitals and even military dining during World War II. Institutions loved these dishes because you could stack them fast and carelessly since they were hard to break.

After the war, American companies marketed plastic dishes to households. They manufactured the brand name of melamine products into modern, space age designs having lustrous surfaces. Industrial and houseware designer Russel Wright created residential pieces with a mottled effect made by overlapping colors, which were given names that read like an exclusive designer catalog: sea mist, lemon ice, copper penny, black velvet and gray. Several tableware companies produced Wright's melamine designs.

Advertisements read, "Quality melamine dinnerware. Candlelight buffet this evening. Family breakfast tomorrow. Patio party this weekend!"

By the late 1980s, Melmac dinnerware had fallen from favor because it became dull and faded from repeated washings. Metal utensils scratched it. Coffee, tea and strongly-colored juices stained the cups. The trend of used decal designs mimicking China patterns looked

151

cheesy and signaled the kiss of death for Melmac. Some dinnerware had hideous flowers in the popular earth tones of the 60s and 70s, which were dried out by the heat of the dishwasher. Yet strangely as it may seem, Melmac is making a comeback in the twenty-first century, especially for outdoor use during spring and summer months. Houseware experts speculate that with the passage of time more melamine will be sold and used throughout the year.

Oddly enough, the inheritance from my mother's house is a huge pink and white speckled platter and turkey roaster that I love! When I use the platter I am reminded of my mother's set of pink Melmac dishes. We also had dishes in that wonderful avocado green.

The Pantry

Old houses often had cubbyhole pantries in the backs of kitchens, since cupboards were rare in those early days. Our pantry had a white-painted table inside that my grandfather made. The shelves of the pantry were lined with flowered Contac paper and stored canned goods, staples, and silverware. The bigger shelves held some of my grandma's turquoise Majolica pottery dishes, several large platters and a cutting board shaped like a pig. There were lots of glassware and plates that my mother had collected over the years. They had been given away as bonuses at movie theaters, gas stations and inside of boxes of laundry detergent. Before any big family get-togethers we had to wash nearly all of them. I never knew what was on the top shelf of the pantry. Maybe that free glass pitcher my mother got for buying twelve bars of Camay soap in all the different colors, or the thermal basketweave

cups and bowls that she got at the dime store.

Inside the pantry was also a small metal linen closet with pink-flowered decals on the doors. My mother kept her linens in this and all the new towels that she rarely used. Her motto was to save everything for good, which was Sunday and for holidays. To this day I have trouble forcing myself to use a new dishtowel.

The Attic

One of my favorite rooms in the house where I grew up was the attic. This huge, unfinished room was fashioned with bare lumber and beams and filled with countless treasures, heirlooms and antiques. Though things that were kept there were valuable only to those connected with the house, I found myself often rummaging through the things, hour after hour, even on hot summer days. It was an escape—a chance to be away from the hubbub of the family. It was a place to dream, and though I didn't know it yet, there were stories here to be told.

Some of my fondest memories were of the visits I made to my mother's house after I grew up, got married and moved away. I anxiously looked forward to the "special" visits with her back in that house on California Street in NE Minneapolis, with its old-fashioned charm and yellowing stucco.

The attic keepsakes I found especially fascinating were my aunt's fashionable Charleston dresses, her high-buttoned shoes, and many colorful hats and purses. My nieces loved dressing up in the bridesmaid dresses that hung beneath plastic. They were made of layers of ruffled pastel chiffon and had nylon picture hats to match. Special heirlooms were stored in her attic, which included my brother and uncle's World War II Army and Navy uniforms and my grandfather's impressive trunk, which he had brought with him across the ocean from Poland in 1903. I also remember the boxes of books that belonged to my aunts and uncles, several rolls of unused wallpaper, numerous family portraits, photo albums, a sentimentally-valuable collection of family letters, cards, newspaper clippings and other memorabilia.

The years have passed and my mother is gone. The house now belongs to someone else. However, some of the nostalgic keepsakes and heirlooms from my mother's attic, which were so much a part of my heritage and childhood years, are now treasures in my own home.

The Basement

My brother and I often played in the basement of our childhood home. A favorite spot to hide was the coal room. We would slip through a small window and jump to the floor. It's funny how kids are attracted to scary spaces. It was dingy and musty. I always had the fear that once I was inside; the door would close and accidentally lock. The basement itself was mysterious. The only way to get there was through the trap door in the center of the back porch. On washdays the door was propped open all day to make it easier for my mother to get to the washing machine downstairs. The fear was always that someone would come by unexpectedly and fall down those stairs. It seemed to me that no one would ever be able to survive that fall.

The crude uneven, concrete steps leading downstairs were sided by a ledge filled with bottles and junk. A quick right turn at the bottom brought a tall shelf that was al-

ways filled with canned goods, pickles, beets and tomatoes into view. Sometimes there were even peaches and pears. To the left of the shelf sat my grandmother's cast iron stove. We always wondered how she got it down there, as it looked massively heavy. They must have built the basement around it. It's probably still there to this day.

Next to the stove was my mother's wringer washer, and on the wall above that was the water meter. I once stood up and conked my head on that monstrous thing. I saw stars for a while. I cannot figure out how I could have stood up and not realized it was there. My head hurt long afterward.

Traditions

A Chore for Every Day

Long ago, the rhythm of the average American housewife's life was fairly standard. Each day had its own task, and so her work got done in a logical, orderly fashion as the week progressed. (Some women still swear by doing housekeeping chores on certain days of the week.)

It went like this: Monday was washday, Tuesday was ironing day. Mending was also done on Tuesday, which made sense, as you'd just been through the clothes and had noticed where a new patch or button was needed. Wednesday was sewing day. Thursday was market day. Friday was cleaning day. Saturday was baking day. And, of course, Sunday was for church and rest.

This was a typical way in which everyone kept house for more than a hundred years. (My mother sometimes varied her routine slightly, doing her baking on Thursday and going to the market Saturday.) It was so common that day-of-the-week dish-towels were everywhere emblazoned with each day's chore (as if you were going to forget!) Usually the dishtowels were embroidered on starched white flour sacks. You can still get Aunt Martha's iron-on transfers that proclaim these daily chores.

The logic behind all of it was that laundry was the heaviest task a housewife had to face. She needed a great deal of strength and fortitude to hand-wring clothes and carry big baskets of wet laundry up the stairs and out to the clothesline from the basement washtubs. On Monday, women were rested and refreshed from Sunday's lack of work. Tuesday's ironing followed Monday's wash, which was also another big job… and so on down the week.

MONDAY WAS WASHDAY. Mom would spend all morning in the basement washing clothes in her Maytag washer. Our basement was only a half basement, accessible by a

trap door. It had a dirt floor, a coal bin, and huge old-fashioned furnace in the middle of the room. The furnace had been added to and updated several times, and metal pipes were going every which way.

Among the cleaning products Mom used were Mrs. Stewart's Bluing and a big bar of Fels Napta soap. Sometimes she would soak stained items in bleach. After washing them she would pull the clothes through the wringer by hand.

I remember Mother caught my favorite dress in the wringer once and ripped it to shreds trying to get it out. I was in junior high then and it had been a hard time in my life anyway. The dress was black-and-white plaid with a red tie at the neck. We had ordered it from the Montgomery Ward catalog. She knew how much I loved that dress, so was afraid to tell me about what had happened. Every time I'd ask about it, she made up some excuse… she hadn't washed it yet or couldn't find it. Then one day she finally told me. Of course, I was broken-hearted. But life did go on.

In the afternoon she would hang all the clothes to dry on the clotheslines in the back yard. I remember the scene well. Starched white sheets would blow in the wind along with stiff towels, jeans and, of course, everyone's underwear for all the world to see. She'd prop the lines with steel poles and her clothespin bag would hang on the end. Sometimes I'd help her hang the clothes or hand her the clothespins. At the end of the day she would take down the fresh-smelling clothes, shake them out, and fold them all into a wicker basket. All of the ladies down our block also hung their clothes out to dry on Mondays.

Most of the houses on the block were alike. Part of a row of clapboard houses, they were so close together they almost touched. These working-class houses of immigrant families had been built by hand tools at the early part of the twentieth century. They had small yards with barely enough room for a sidewalk between them. Many had the exact same style porch that was lined with windows across the front.

The habits of all these neighbors were very much

alike. If you didn't hang your clothes to dry the neighbors would ask about it, thinking something was wrong. My mother hung her clothes in the basement when it rained or during the winter. "The clothes wouldn't dry" seemed to come into every conversation she had.

TUESDAY WAS IRONING DAY. The place reserved for ironing was always on one end of the kitchen nearest to the telephone. There would be a basket of clothes and a sprin-kling bottle on top of the ironing table. Our sprinkler was an old Orange Nesbitt pop bottle with a metal cap that had holes punched in it. I used to watch my mother iron for hours. She made it look easy. One day I asked if I could try. I did a terrible job. It took forever to iron one shirt and it still looked wrinkled after I was done with it. What I didn't know was that there was a certain trick. In those days, fabrics were different. There was more cotton and it was a stiffer more wrinkly type. Sprinkling water on them kept them moist. You couldn't soak the garment, but it had to be wet enough to take out the wrinkles. My mother had done it so often that she knew the exact amount to spray on. White cotton shirts with collars and cuffs were probably the hardest to do and what I had chosen for my first ironing project. No easy piece for me, such as a small, flat hanky. Instructions were to lay the garment out on the table, sprinkle it and all the others, one by one, roll them tightly, return them to the basket, then cover the

basket with a towel. This kept the clothes wet enough for ironing. If they couldn't be finished that day, you could sprinkle the clothes, roll them, wrap them in Saran Wrap and refrigerate.

WEDNESDAY WAS BREAD-BAKING DAY. I remember the rows of baked bread cooling on the kitchen table or in the pantry. Growing up with so many kids in our family, we never really had an abundance of material things. But we always had homemade bread and sometimes apple pie or donuts. The pies were made using apples from our next-door neighbor, Mrs. Kubinski. I remember how good the bread tasted, still warm from the oven, spread with creamy butter and homemade jam. How wonderful the house smelled when the bread was baking. Sometimes my brothers and sisters and I were allowed to make little dough shapes of our own and sprinkle them with cinnamon and sugar. I usually cut mine with a Santa cookie cutter.

When I was very young, on the occasional donut-making days, we each had our own donut bag, which was a brown paper bag filled with donuts, donut holes and cookie-cutter shapes. One time, my brother got up in the middle of the night and for some strange reason went to one side of his bedroom and peed into his donut bag. We laughed as we told that story for years.

Friday was cleaning day. We usually had a lot of company on the weekends so I suppose that's why my mother cleaned on Friday. She swept, dusted, waxed the floors and beat the rugs on the line. "Don't step on the linoleum floor, it's not dry yet," she often said, and, "Hang up your coat; were you born in a barn?" Those were the sayings I grew up with.

Christmas When I was Growing Up

Christmas was always a special time for our family. Mistletoe hung in specially chosen places each year and cards were taped all over the walls and on the woodwork and mirrors. We sprayed snowy glitter on the windows and as the holiday approached, our house became a beehive of activity: cleaning, shopping and cooking. Everything was overdone and we loved it.

Visitors stopped by to wish us a Merry Christmas and all of my older married brothers and sisters came with their children. We would exchange a few gifts, but mostly had a good time talking, dancing and singing. We ate ham, polish sausages, pierogis and galapkis. The favorite bread was poppy seed, and of course we ate lots of Christmas cookies that my aunt had spent days making. Everyone was happy. There was lots of chatter as the record player in the kitchen played carols in the background. My favorite part as a child was after the ladies had cleared the table and done the dishes. Then everyone would retire into the living room where we sang carols around the piano. Sometimes my aunts and uncles would sing their favorite oldies, and of course, my Uncle Joe would always chant "Dzie Bethlehem" in Polish!

There was a feeling about that night that was almost

indescribable. We children would form a circle around the Christmas tree and sing "Silent Night." It always made me tear up as I stared at the star on top of the tree and remembered the first star of Bethlehem. There was a sense of wonder tied in with the night Jesus was born and no matter how things really were in our lives—on that night there was peace on earth. We all went to Midnight Mass then, which I loved. It was the one night of the year where we got to stay up late. We were dressed in our new outfits and sang more songs, while everyone in the congregation held a lighted candle. It was a beautiful sight and once again I believed that on Christmas Eve any miracle could happen.

A Fifties Christmas

Christmas in the fifties was an important event. Families celebrated together and traditions started that are still with many families today. One of the most sacred traditions at Christmas was the decorating of the tree. This usually involved a variety of different ornaments, tinsel, and of course, the all-important star. Some ornaments were homemade while others were bought at the Five & Dime, Woolworth's, or even Sears.

Popular ornaments for that period were made of glass, feathers, hand-painted wood, paper and plastic. Fragile glass ornaments were molded or blown. A popular inexpensive type was the Shiny Brite brand. Thousands of these ornaments were sold at prices so low that most families could afford them. The more expensive blown-glass ornaments usually came from overseas.

The feathered bird ornaments were sometimes quite elaborate. Real feathers were added for the wings and tail. Wooden miniature ornaments were prized because of the time and work that had gone into making them. They were often unique.

Some families could not afford expensive ornaments and would buy or make them out of paper. The store-bought varieties had die cut shapes printed with wonderful lithographs in bright colors. Chains to go around the tree were made of popcorn, cranberries and red and green construction paper. For a time, crocheted and stringed ornaments were popular. Yarn or string could be wrapped around a ball or any object, then sprayed with starch and glitter.

Plastic ornaments were another inexpensive way to decorate. Those wonderful ornaments were made in every shape and size, ranging from nativity scenes to angels and Santa Claus. They were very cheap and durable. Most families had some form of plastic ornaments in their Christmas decoration box.

Tree lights in those days were of the old-fashioned large smooth or ribbed cone kind, in primary colors. When one light burned out, the whole string stopped working. Bubble lights were great and we were fascinated by them, but they never seemed to last very long. We wondered what was in that small chamber that produced the bubbling liquid. The "fairy" or miniature lights debuted in the early 1950s and became the accepted form of Christmas light by the mid 1980s. They remain popular today.

The star was the most honored tree ornament and was put on top of the tree very carefully at the end of decorating to remind us of the night Jesus was born. We also made a wish at that time.

Hanig family Christmas, 1961

During the fifties cellophane window wreaths were very popular. The earliest wreath was made of chenille and later ones were made of sparkling cellophane. A red cellophane wreath with a cream-colored electric candle in the center was also a traditional choice to have in the window, harking back to the days when a red rose was put in the window at Christmas. On rare occasions these wreaths can still be found in antique stores.

Tree tinsel had to be applied piece by piece. There was no other way. It took a long time to apply unless you had help. My brother always took the short cut and threw tinsel on all at once, and the results mirrored the lack of effort: It looked like a messy glob.

As styles of decorations change through the years we may find ourselves longing again for the Christmas tree of old where each decoration had meaning and was cherished.

Remember Aluminum Christmas Trees?

In 1959, a toy salesman for the Aluminum Specialty Company noticed a homemade all-metal tree on display in a Ben Franklin Five and Dime store in Chicago. He presented this new version of a Christmas tree to his company right away and the design department came up with an idea. At the time Manitowoc, Wisconsin, was known as the Aluminum Cookware Capital of the World. By Christmas of 1959, the very first all-aluminum Christmas tree was presented to the public. Surprisingly, the idea took off and by 1960 the company had perfected the Evergleam. They produced about four million trees from 1959 to 1969.

The company advertised their trees as a "Permanent Tree." It had a silver painted wooden trunk with holes drilled in angles up to the top, so that when branches were inserted they would fold upwards and give the shape of a traditional tree. Equipped with a tripod style stand, the trees were easy to set up and shimmered brightly like tinsel.

They became so popular that imitators copied the design, and the market was flooded with a variety of aluminum; not only in original silver, but also gold, green, blue, pink, a combination of blue and green, and one that was silver with blue tips. The aluminum branches conducted electricity and it was dangerous to decorate the tree with electric lights, so rotating multicolored floodlights were sold to shine on the trees for illumination. The companies  offered a wide variety of these color-wheels. Trees stood as tall as 7 feet and there were even tabletop trees.

Public interest started to fade after December of 1965 when they became a symbol of commercialism on a Charlie Brown Christmas special that aired on CBS. Charlie Brown refused to buy one when Lucy instructed him to get "the biggest aluminum tree he could find, maybe even painted pink." The heart of America followed. By 1968 most companies no longer sold aluminum trees.

Memories of Christmases Past

Betty Kieley

When the three of us were growing up our whole lives revolved around the church. My best friend Geri, my sister Carolyn and me were always together. No one had a lot of money and it was the purest time of my life. That was before the world became corrupted. We looked forward to Christmas time; it was a special event in our lives. Prior to the Christmas pageant we drew names amongst our Sunday School classmates. You never knew who had your name and there was such anticipation surrounding it; whispering and excitement.

There were so few in our class that we always had a guaranteed part in the play. We didn't have costumes but there would be a small stage that looked like Bethlehem and always a huge star above it. At the end we sang carols. We looked forward to the end of the pageant when we would all go down to the church basement for cookies, lemonade and of course to exchange our gifts . We were each given a small square box tied with a string [shaped like animal cracker box] and it was filled with ribbon candy. It was the Best Night; times were hard and we knew there were not a lot of presents at home for us.

Betty Kieley, Carolyn Cederberg, and Geri Peterson, 1950

Super 6 taken at Frank Dattalo's Coon Rapids home. Getting ready for the GSTA State Rod and Custom Show 50th Anniversary.

Chapter 12

Classic Cars and Drag racing

Hot Rod Fever

There was nothing as cool as a hot rod in a teenager's life. A car meant freedom and a proud social standing. The appeal of the souped up car was pretty universal for teenage males. Speed and self-expression was part of the 1950s hot rod fever. If you could get yourself a junkyard jalopy and transform it into daily transportation or even use it for racing, (a girl-getting machine), you'd have it made.

Drag racing has been done for decades, but it reached new heights in the 1950s. Some teenagers competed in official races, but most of the time they dragged the streets. If a guy was sitting at a stoplight in his roadster and another guy came up in a fine machine with its engine roaring, they both waited for someone to utter the magic words, "Want to drag?" Then, the light would turn green and off they would roar.

Most guys in those days didn't have much money, so the challenge was to take a run-down, beat-up car and turn it into a sleek, rubber-burning machine. 'Change everything on it you could' was usually the motto. So, every evening and weekend many guys devoted themselves to one thing; working on their car.

The specialty shops supplied all the add-ons and magazines like Rod and Custom and Hot Rod offered all sorts of ideas and know-how. In the late 1950s, the artistry of fixing up a car became the new craze. The new lingo included words like: rake, flathead, bent eight, blow off, chop, drop, three on the tree.

The drive-in burger joint was the hot-rodder's hang out. It was a place to show off cars, meet new girls and issue drag invitations. Life was all about racing. Sometimes a drag was no more than two guys revving it up at a red light. But often it could involve a hundred hot-rodders that would turn a section of less-traveled road into a drag strip. It was a noisy place with engines revving, rock and roll music blaring and teens cheering. A dangerous sport, cops responded with raids and tickets for speeding, inadequate safety equipment and for creating a public nuisance. Accidents soared and there was talk of outlawing those 'killing machines driven by crazy delinquents.' Safety-conscious clubs were formed by the police department and encouraged by concerned citizens.

The sport became so popular that in 1956 there were 130 legal drag strips in forty states across the country. In most cases the strips were half-mile sections of unused airplane runway, but in some places

1957 Ford Fairlane

1955 Chev

the police closed off a section of a city street for twice-monthly drag races. The souped up, stripped down cars blasted off, two by two, in quarter-mile elimination heats and drivers that were able to last through the afternoon earned the title of "Top Eliminator" in their class. Each winner was rewarded with a trophy and kiss from a pretty girl.

The difference between the 1950 and 1960's car was that in the 50s young guys didn't have much money to spend, so they built their own cars. In the 60s, there was more opportunity for teens to earn money and buy cars—hence, the arrival of the Muscle Car.

Popular Cars of the 50s

1. 55 Chev
2. 56 Chev
3. 57 Chev
4. Ford Fairlane

5. Pontiac 2 door
6. Olds Rocket 88
7. 49 Mercury
8. 40 Ford Coup
9. Thunderbird [parents]
10. Studebaker [parents]

Muscle Cars of the 1960s

The very words American Muscle Car speaks of automotive power. To some, the Muscle Car era was the greatest period in automotive history, lasting from 1960 to 1972. During this period, Detroit created the greatest performance machine of all time by following an age-old recipe: place a big engine in a relatively small car and put it at a price the average person can afford. True muscle cars followed the adages, "There is no substitute for cubic inches," and "There is no replacement for displacement." This resulted in some truly remarkable

Muscle Car Songs

409 • The Beach Boys
Little Deuce Coupe • The Beach Boys
Shut Down • The Beach Boys
The Little Old Lady From Pasadena • Jan and Dean
Dead Man's Curve • Jan and Dean
GTO • Ronny and the Daytonas
Hey Little Cobra • The Rip Chords

vehicles. The glorious Muscle Car era is a trip back to the glory days of the American automobile.

Perhaps the most common question people have today about them is, "What exactly is a muscle car?" The term wasn't used until the late 1970s, as in the 1960s they were often called Super Cars or had no delineation at all. Therefore, the actual definition of a muscle car, or even which model was a muscle car, is a topic that is often disputed. Here is the general interpretation: A muscle car by the strictest definition is an intermediate size, performance-oriented model that is powered by a large V8 engine at an affordable price. Most of these models were based on a "regular" production vehicle. The definition includes only intermediate-sized vehicles, whereas in reality, performance-oriented, intermediate size didn't appear until 1964. Before then, manufacturers took existing full-sized vehicles and added extra performance to them. Because of this, the early full-size performance vehicles were generally considered muscle cars. In addition

to full size and intermediate muscle cars, a number of smaller vehicles started appearing on the automotive performance scene. The new "pony cars" and compact cars were considered Muscle Cars only if they contained top-of-the-line performance engines and options.

Pontiac GTO

The Pontiac GTO is considered the first true muscle car. When other manufacturers were concentrating on their full-size lines, Pontiac saw the potential for dropping a big block engine into an intermediate frame and marketed it at a budget price. They sneaked past the GM restriction by making the GTO an option on the Tempest model, which created the hottest performance  machine yet. The GTO sold in great numbers and fueled the competition between GM, Ford and Chrysler that kept the muscle car industry thriving for years. They stopped making the GTO in 1974. It has since come back.

Ford Mustang

Intermediate-sized muscle cars with big block engines were gradually replacing full-sized muscle cars when Lee Iacocca, Ford's General Manager, envisioned a small sports car that would be the next hot item in the street wars. Ford decided that instead of improving its lackluster intermediate, they would do the competition one better and introduce a whole new breed of automo-

be equipped with several V8s and a myriad of performance options. Chevrolet stated that the Camaro was named after the French word for "comrade" although some linguists argued that it was actually Spanish for a type of shrimp. The Camaro was available from the start in hardtop coupes and convertible body styles. It could be ordered with nearly eighty factory options and forty dealer accessories, with a choice of four different engines. Of greater interest to the enthusiast was the SS package, which included standard equipment, a modified 350 cid V8 along with simulated air-intakes on the hood, special bumble bee striping and a blacked-out grill. It was possible to order both the RS and SS packages. Camaro popularity soared when a RS/SS Convertible with the 396 paced the 1967 Indianapolis 500 race.

bile: the pony car. The Ford Mustang was introduced as a 1965 model based on the compact Falcon, which had lower production costs. The date was April 17, 1964. Iacocca realized the Mustang's true success would depend upon its volume sales. It came with an obligatory back seat and multitude of options that gave the buyer an opportunity to better customize his purchase and generate extra profit for the company. The Plymouth Car Company faithfully stressed that their Barracuda beat the Ford Mustang to market by two weeks, but it was the Mustang that racked up over 22,000 sales in its first day and one million sales after two years. The pony class car that the Mustang inspired is the only class of muscle car that still exists today.

Z28 Camaro

In December 1966, Chevrolet quietly released one of the most famous option codes of all time, the option Z-28. Unpublicized and not known by most of the pub-

Chevrolet Camaro

After the success of Ford's Mustang, General Motors finally launched its entry into the pony car race with the Chevrolet Camaro. The Camaro could

lic or Chevrolet salesmen, it was not mentioned in sales literature anywhere. The only way someone could order it was when they were qualifying it to be raced. It came with a competition suspension and broad racing stripes on the hood and trunk lid. There was no Z-28 badge that attracted attention. This car proved difficult to launch on the street because its high-revving engine was lethargic under 4000 rpm and worked best when it was shifted at 7500 rpm! Once it got going though, the Z28 was tough to beat and boasted of a 140 mph top speed that gave it numerous racing victories. Only six hundred and two Z-28s were sold in 1967, making it a truly desirable collectable.

Chevelle SS

The Chevelle SS represented Chevrolet's entry into the hot mid-sized muscle car battle. It was the company's high performance version that had its own line of engines and performance equipment. The first engine was just a 327 V8. The next was a powerful 396 V8, and eventually, the LS6 454 in 1970 would be rated the most power-

ful engine in muscle car history. The Chevelle, along with the Pontiac GTO, remains one of the most popular cars from that era. With good reason too, as it's strong performance and reasonable price made it popular at the track. The hot Chevelle SS for 1965 was the limited edition

List of Muscle Cars

AMC Javelin	Galaxie 390
Buick GS	Mustang GT
Chevrolet	Mercury
Camaro SS and Z28	Comet/Cyclone
Chevelle SS	Couger
Impala SS	Oldsmobile 442
Nova	Plymouth
Dodge	'Cudas
Challenger	Duster
Coronet R/T	GTX,
Charger R/T	Road Runner
Dart	Superbird
Daytona	Pontiac Catalina
Super Bee	2+2
Ford FairlaneTorino	Firebird
GT Cobra	GTO

396, known as the Z-16 package. Only two hundred one of these 375 bhp bruisers were made, 200 hardtops and 1 convertible, and all had stouter convertible-type frames, beefed-up suspensions, front and rear anti-roll bars and faster power-assisted steering. A Muncie 4-speed with axle ratios as high as 4.56:1, was available instead of the standard model. It would take another year before the 396 would be available to the masses and then, the Chevelle SS would be transformed into a true muscle car.

Cruisin' and Racin' in the Fifties

Frank Dattalo

Frank worked for the City of Minneapolis in the Equipment Division for thirty years. He is now a semi-retired real estate broker. Frank's friend Carl Finney works with my husband. Carl and Frank raced together for 25 years and still are good friends. He now owns Hotheads by Frank in Coon Rapids where he works on high performance cylinder heads and sells speed equipment. He still works on cars as a hobby and builds replicas of old cars with car kits.

Frank Dattalo has always loved cars. According to him he's been playing with them every since he was eighteen years old and building them since he was twenty-two years old in 1964. When he was very small he would take all his toys apart to see what made them tick. His Dad said he'd rather play with tools then his own toys. These are some of his memories.

In the summer of 1957 I was bored out of my mind. So I went up to the school library where I saw something that would change my life forever, a copy of *Hot Rod* magazine. My mother worked for Donaldson's in the Accounts Payable Department at the time. I called and asked her if she could pick me up a copy of *Hot Rod* magazine. I still have my first copy, the September issue of 1957 that cost 25 cents. Since then I have collected over 4000 magazines. While I read my magazines I would study and dream of some day building my first hot rod.

Earlier that year I had just turned fifteen and got my first job. My godfather gave me a job making pizzas at his restaurant called the Lido Café in St. Paul. My pay was 95 cents an hour to start and I worked every Friday and Saturday nights. Wow! Money I could save for a car. But Dad said I couldn't get a car until I graduated from high school. So I kept buying *Hot Rod* magazines and dreaming that someday I would buy my own car. Then I started an account with Farmers and Mechanics Bank, a school savings program and I saved something every week. I told my friend George that some day I was going to buy a car.

My friends and I would meet at Porky's Drive-In on University Avenue in St. Paul. Often on the weekend we would cruise all the drive-ins during the evening. But we all had to pitch in for gas. It was the three of us: Bob, George and I. We'd talk about cars and look for some drag racing action on the street. Sometimes it was just from stop sign to stop sign. On Friday and Saturday nights during the winter we'd go out to the Sun Drive in on Central Avenue and then out to the Lake Street drive-ins. We'd grab a pop and see who was there and talked cars. When we got older some guys would have a beer and try to pick up girls. Prior to owning my own car my father Tony would let me use the family car for cruising and dates. One night I decided to take Dad's 1959 Chevy to the Twin City Drag Strip and raced it. I didn't win, the car was a dog. Several years later Dad told me he knew I raced the '59 Chevy; the guys from his work saw the car out at the track and told him about it.

In 1958 we started a car club called the Drover Auto Club of Minneapolis. We had jackets and car plaques. We would display the car plaques in the back window shelf or under the rear bumper. The plaque could not hang from a chain. We had as many as ten members in the club, guys from school and the neighborhood. We had a car club advisor whose name was Leo Kirkbride. He was a member of the Optimist Club that was responsible for building Minnesota Drag Ways in Coon Rapids. It was on Highway 242 right in the middle of nowhere. They wanted to get drag racing off the streets and organize it. At the time it cost 50 cents to watch the races. We had lots of friends racing. Coon Rapids has always been called the "heart of hot rod country." Even today many people that reside in Coon Rapids are still building cars. The drag strip is gone now. Urban sprawl took its toll on it.

In June of 1960, I graduated from North High School in Minneapolis. But it was in the spring of the year I started to drive my dad nuts about buying a car. I had been planning on buying a 1960 Chevrolet Biscayne 2 Door with a 348 cubic inch motor, 4 speed transmission and a 335 H.P. engine. It had 4.11 positraction axle and a manual radio.

But Dad said, "Why don't you buy yourself a Chevrolet convertible?" [He didn't want me drag racing.] Well, then I gave in and ordered a red convertible with a white top, and red and white interior. I ordered a 348 cubic inch, 250 horse power motor, with a 3 speed transmission [3 in the tree] and 3.70 positraction axle and manual radio. List price was $3480.00 and with the discount I paid $2800.00. Tony Sticka was the salesman at Midway Chrevrolet, where we had purchased other cars. I had hung around there often. I ordered the car on March 23rd, 1960, and had estimated the build time of six weeks. I drove poor Tony nuts for several weeks, looking to find out the exact date the car would be built. I

Top – 55 Chevy later became Super 6
Middle – 1961 Turquoise Chevy Hard top
Bottom – Frank with his first car; the original 60 Chevy Convertible. Taken at his graduation dinner at the Buckhorn Restaurant in Wisconsin 1960.

Top – 1956 Chevy Convertible, Sierra Tan and
Adobe Beige two-tone

Middle – 1969 Chevy Nova

Bottom – 1960 Chevy Convertible

called him every day.

On May 3, 1960, I knew the car had been built. So I went down to the train yards where the cars came in on freight trains. Wow! I found it and was it beautiful! I jumped up and down with excitement. There was no one with me so what. Oh, I forgot I ordered a tinted green windshield. That's how I could tell it was my car. Plus I read the build sheet affixed to the side window with the description of the build. Then I went straight over to the dealership to tell Tony the car was in and when could I get it? He said I could pick it up on Wednesday. [I'm sure he was relieved that I wouldn't be bugging him any more.]

When I got the car home I wanted to install some gauges on it-water temp, oil gauge, and tachometer. My mother had a fit. She told my Dad Tony, "He's taking his new car apart."

The day after graduation I took the car over to Champion Auto to get Sneaker drag pipes welded to the exhaust ahead of the mufflers. [You could open them up at the drag strip so you could get more horsepower out of the engine when they were uncapped.] That next Friday night Twin City Drag Strip was open, so my brother Jim and I took my new car out to the drag strip when it only had 600 miles on it.

Shortly after I started going out to the drag strip I started winning trophies and I'd sneak them home and hide them in my closet in shoe boxes. One night I brought my father to the grocery store and when he got in the car he asked me if my car was for sale.

I said "No, why do you ask?"

"Well," he said, "I saw lettering on the windshield that looks like it's for sale." What it was is the class I was drag racing in was stamped on the windshield. When I left the track I would wipe the white shoe polish off the windshield and it left a stain.

My brother Jim said, "You better tell Dad you're drag racing."

So after supper I went and got the trophies and gave them to my Dad while he was sitting in his easy chair watching TV and he hollered, "Mary, he's racing his new car."

Every Wednesday or Friday night my mother would meet me at the back door when I got home and I'd have to hide the trophy under my jacket when I came in. When she turned her back I would add the trophy to the top of the breakfront where the other trophies were displayed. The next morning she'd be looking at her glassware and she'd look up and exclaim, "Tony, he been racing again!"

In late 1960, I met a gal and she didn't like me drag racing my new cars. She sided with Ma and Dad. So I quit drag racing. But the bug was never far away. In 1963 we got married and purchased a home. In the spring of 1964 we had our first son, Frank Jr. My friend Bob and I always talked about going drag racing again. So the plan was put into place. Our wives could not complain if we didn't race our everyday cars, so we were going to buy a car just for racing.

We bought a cheap 1955 Chevrolet 2 Door Sedan from Belair Motors on Lake Street. It cost $65.00 plus $2.00 for the title transfer. Bob and I split the cost. The car was rusty and someone had painted it with a paint brush; white on the top and green on the lower body. It was a straight 6 cylinder engine with a 3 on the tree transmission and no battery. The owner said we had to get it out of there right away, so we pushed it backward down the alley and popped the clutch to get it started. We got the car almost home when it stopped running. A driver came by and said, "What's the matter?" and I said, "I think the pilot light went out."

We took it over to my father's house to put it in the garage. [I did not have a garage at the time]. He saw the car and said, "Frankie, what are you going to do with that piece of junk?"

I said, "I'm going to build a drag car."

Then he said, "You should take it to the junk yard." He just shook his head and walked away.

It took seven years to build that car. We didn't have much money at that time. I would spend $3.00 a week for supplies. My take home pay was only $65.00 a week. We started doing body work and all the magazines were starting to pay off. I was teaching myself how to use Bondo. The gaps over the headlights were so big it took window screening with newspaper and of course Bondo to fill it in. A block of wood, a piece of 80 grit sandpaper and desire were my tools. A friend of my wife came to the rescue and loaned me a body shop grinder. It really helped. It took all summer. My father would come out in the garage and watch me work on my car and kept me in water. Bob had a friend who let us use an electric spray gun so we could spray some primer on it for the winter.

The next spring we got the body ready for painting and a friend gave us a gallon of orange paint. All we had to do is find someone to paint it. Such a guy surfaced that would paint it for $50.00 if we had it all masked, taped and tacked clean. When the car was done we had to take it right home. His shop was in the Bryn Mar area where he painted cars in a Quonset hut. When the car was painted we hooked up the tow bar for the trip home, and one block from home it started to rain. We did get it in the garage before any damage was done. The next morning my Dad called and said he had seen the car at Bob's house when he was taking the paper and tape off and it really looked good.

We had the body done and now we needed an engine. We wanted something different and decided on a six cylinder engine. A book by Frank McGurk and GMC by Bill Fisher became our guide. We built a 302 GMC motor out of an army truck and we named the car, "Super Six." I designed the intake manifold that had 2X4BBLS carburetors and high rise log design. With help from friends we welded it all up. Many people said it would not work, but we proved them wrong.

After we got it built we started to take it out to the drags to work out the bugs. Soon we were winning our class and having fun. Everyone liked the car because it was unique. Everyone else was running Chevy V8's and we were running an incline 6 cylinder with 320 cubic inches 4 speed transmission and 4.56 positraction rear end with slicks. She did turn heads.

Our first car show was the G.S.T.A. Rod and Custom Show. We were chosen for the spring of 1969 show. And guess who was there? Yep! My Dad was so proud. He stood and looked at the car and told people the story that went with it. What a guy! He was really a great Dad. He never went to the drag strips to watch us race, but he always called to see how we did. Just a note, that Super Six was invited back to the G.S.T.A. Show for their 50th Anniversary on April 1st, 2006 and it was a hit.

In 1974 I partnered with my father and built a 1956 Chevrolet Bel Air Convertible. No, he did not work on it but he put money and support into the project and attended the car shows with it. It took me 6 months to build.

Since the beginning I have acquired many tools and everything I needed to build a car. I have gone to trade schools at night to learn the different skills needed. Welding, engine tuning, carburetor rebuilding, apprenticed cylinder head rebuilding, and self taught cylinder head porting. I have also helped build each of my son's cars. Frank Jr. has a 1969 and 1972 Camaro, and a 1967 Chevelle convertible. Dan has a 1965 and 1970 Chevelle and a 1965 Nova.

Hotheads by Frank

My love for cars and hobby of building them has inspired me to help and guide other people who are interested in cars to pursue their dreams. In the 1980s while working a regular full time job to support my family, I decided to start a company called Hot Heads by Frank. It is a shop that does Hi Performance Cylinder Head Work on engines. Since the start we have expanded to sell speed equipment to help increase the performance of these engines. In our weekly ads we have a telephone number listed so auto enthusiasts can call with questions and concerns.

Since my retirement from my regular job in 1994, I have expanded the Hotheads Company and it has supplemented my income so I could continue building my cars. I just finished building a 1932 Ford Roadster that took 6 years to build. I have just started on my last project—a 1941 Willys, that will be a supercharged motor car and should make near 1000 HP. My grandson Anthony is coming of age and I'm looking forward to teaching him the craft of building hot rods.

Car Clubs

Gopher State Timing Assn., Cogs, Lone Wolfs, Drovers, 3-2 Relics, Cruisers, Nights, Beater Boys, Quads, Street Customs, Strokers, Golden Rods, Universals, Igniters, Long Lake Roadsters Club, and Minnesota Street Rod Assn.

Car Parts and Gear

Fancy hub caps, wide white wall tires, porta walls [white wall inserts], lake pipes, tear drop spot lights, dual exhaust with smithy mufflers, lowering blocks, fuzzy dice hanging from your inside mirror, fender skirts, 3X2BBL and 2X4BBLS carburetors, 6X2"S carburetors on log manifolds, flat head Ford V8, Small Chevy V8 (265-283 Cu.In.motor),

4 speed transmission, positraction axel, 4.11 gears, slicks [drag tires], car club placques and jackets, tachometers, and gauges.

Some of the Cars I've Had

1930 Ford Pick Up Builder
1947 Chev 2 Dr Sedan Builder
1955 Chev 4 Dr Wagon Builder
1956 Chev Convertible 2nd Builder
1956 Ford Fairlane 2 Dr Hard top Builder
1957 Chev 210 2 Dr Sedan
1960 Chev Convertible #1in High School
1960 Chev Convertible #2 Built
1961 Chev Impala 2 Dr Hard top 1st
1964 Malibu Super Sport 2 Dr Hard top
1968 Chev Impala 2 Dr Hard top
1969 Chev Nova 2 Dr Sedan Builder
1967 Chev RS Camaro
1964 Chevelle Malibu Convertible Builder

Cars I Still Have in My Collection

1932 Ford Roadster Builder
1941 Willys 2 Dr Builder
1955 Chev 2 Dr Sedan (SUPER SIX)
1956 Chev Bel Air Convertible
1961 Chev Impala 2 Dr Hard top 2nd 409 Motor Car
2002 Chev Avalanche 4 Dr SUV 4X4
2005 Chrysler 300 Limited 4 Dr. Touring

A Photographic Stroll Down Memory Lane

Paper Dolls & Toys from the 50s

A Fifties Christmas

Patterns and Sewing

Family and Activities

The Sattler Family Home made Circle Skirts 1955

Pam in a plastic covered chair

Christmas Pam's Family 1950s

A Game of Badminton 1956

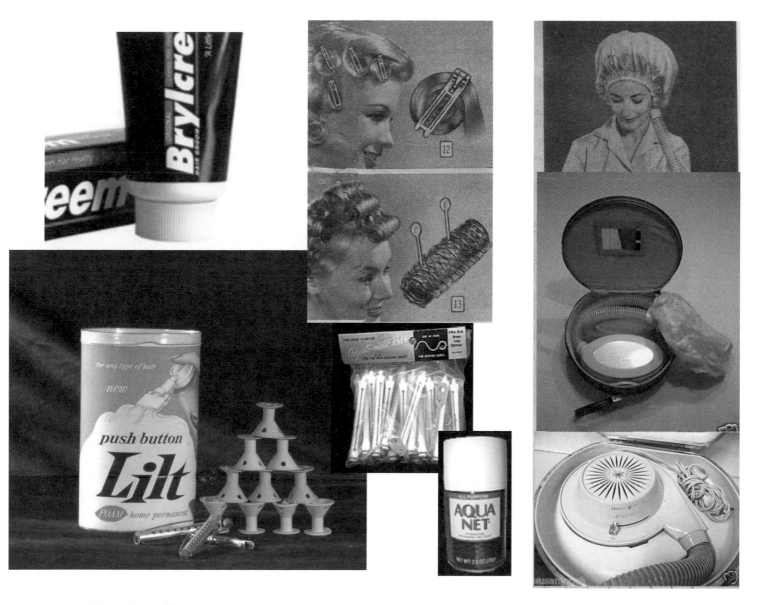

Hair Care in the 50s and 60s Home Perms, Bobby pins, Spoolies and Aqua Net Hair Spray

1950s and 60s Cars

1] 1957 Ford Fairlane owned by Roger Davidson, 2] 1953 Mercury owned by Frank & Mary Jo King, 3] 1965 Chevy II Nova owned by Tom Fournier, 4] 1969 Yellow Ford Mustang owned by Mike Hinkemeyer, 5] 1969 Chevy Camaro owned by Steve Thornton, 6] 1956 Peach Ford. All cars on this page are from Buffalo Car Show September 2008.

Cars from the 50s and 60s

1] 1957 Thunderbird owned by Rhonda Cottrell, 2] 1957 Pink Chevy owned by Barb & Pete Sargeant, 3] 1970 Blue Chevelle SS owned by Dan & Julie Martin, 4] 1968 El Camino Yenko owned by Gordon Frolik, 5] 1969 Silver Buick Grand Sport

Remember the Northern Girls

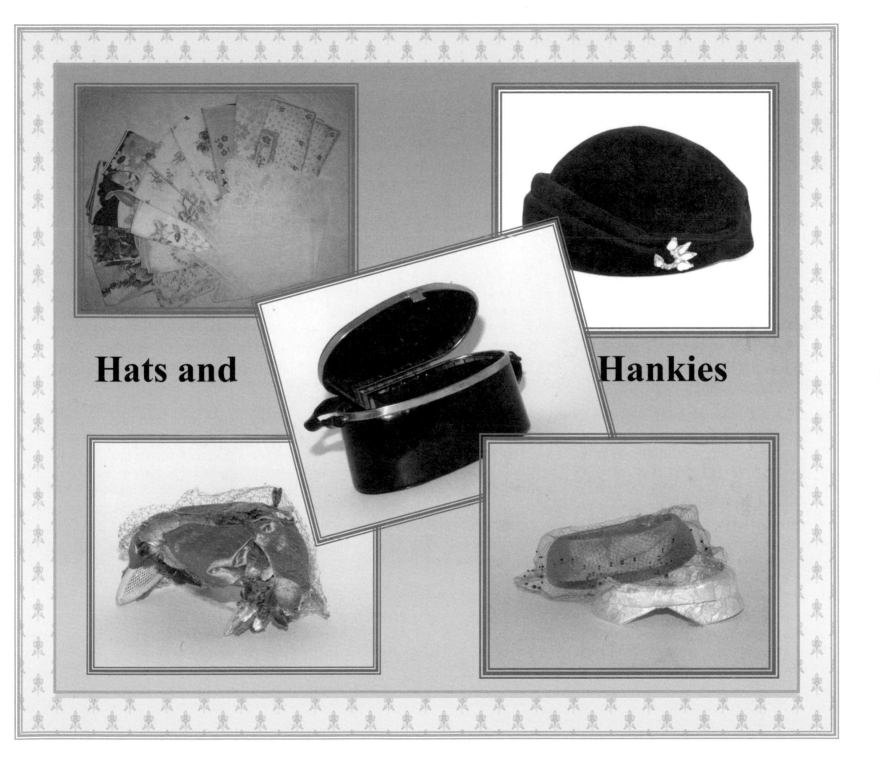

Hats and Hankies

Band Members

Joker's Wild 1967—Bill Jordan, Pete Huber, Lonnie Knight, Denny Johnson & Greg Springer

Musical Theater Company Band with Wolfman Jack 1976—Bruce Arneson, Mike Gulenchyn, Kevin Sylvers and Randy Arneson at Astroworld in Houston, TX.

One of the longest running groups in the Twin Cities.

Del Counts 1976--Al Miller, Charlie Schoen, Mike Kryduba, Chris Castenada, Steve Miller at Mr. Nibs.

Del Counts 1968—original group Bill LaFave, Bill Saley, Thom Aspinwall & Charlie Schoen.

Underbeats 1968—Rico Rasenbaum, Tom Nystrom, Jim Johnson and Don Larsen.

Chancellors 1960s—David Rivkin, John Hughes, Mike Judge & Dan Holm

Trashmen 1960s—Steve Wahrer, Bob Reed, Tony Andreason & Dal Winslow.

High Spirits 1964-69—Doug Ahrens, Rick Beresford, Bob Cohen, Owen Husney, Rick Levinson, Jay Luttio, Frank Prout, David Rivkin, & Cliff Siegel.

Band Photos Page 128 Benilde Year Book 1966, 1967 & 1968, 130 Courtesy of Randy Arneson, 130 Courtesy of Charlie Schoen, 128-129 Music Legends: A Rewind on the Minnesota Music Scene by Martin Keller

Downtown & Dime Stores

Scenes of Old Donaldson's--90 First floor lunch counter-Donaldson's- St. Paul 1951, Donaldson's Food Fair 1950s, Crowd of Donaldson's Dollar Day sale Mpls.1957. Christmas Decorations with Church on window 1940s, 91 Dayton's Department Store 1915, 59 Dayton's hat display window 1957, 96 J C Penney's Store 1958, 101 Amluxen's 1975, 102 Nankin Café 1958, 107 View from balcony

interior of Forum 1953, 105 Forum Cafeteria 1953, 113 F. W. Woolworth Store 1955, 94--Dayton's Teen Board members--Joanne Cheney, Karen Lee, Barbara Rowan & Pam Albinson

138 & 172 -- Courtesy of General Mills

150, 154, 155 & cover inset—Special thanks to Elaine Farniok for her generosity and fine embroidered Day of the Week dish towels from Annie's Attic Antique Shop in Buffalo, MN

176 Courtesy of Pam Velander

Index of Subjects

A & W Root Beer-80
American Bandstand-22
Amluxen's &Learning to Sew/Joannie Moses-38
Amluxen's-101
Aprons-60-63
Attic, the Basement, the Pantry-152-153
Autograph Albums-148
Baldies and Greasers-33
Beatles on the Ed Sullivan Show-122
Beehive-54
Ben Casey Shirt/Blouse-42
Betty Crocker Coupons-138
Bras, Nylons and Girdles-48-49
Breck Girl-55
Bridgeman's-81
Catalogs-147
Cereal Box Prize-148
Chandler Shoes-100
Charm Bracelets-42
Chevrolet Camaro-164
Child of the 50s-6
Christmas When I was Growing Up-156
Chore for Every Day—Monday Wash Day-153
Closing the Dime Stores: The End of an Era-117
Cowboy Shows, Monster Movies, and Playing Ball
    in the Streets / Doug Kieley-15
Crinolines-41
Cruisin & Racin' in the Fifties/Frank Dattalo-166
Culottes-45
Day John F. Kennedy was Shot-121
Day of the Week Panties-142

Dayton's 8th Floor Auditorium-Christmas-92
Daytons-91
Depression Glass-139
Do you remember these Songs of the '50s?-124
Donaldson's Glass Block-89
Empire-Waist Dresses-45
Evening in Paris Perfume-143
F & M School Savings Program-17
Fashion1950s AmericanBandstand Standards-31
Fashion in the 1960s-33
Fashion Memories from 50s/Nancy O'Dette-34
Fashion Sewing in the 1960s-37
Fifties Christmas-157
First Home Permanents-55
Ford Mustang-163
Forum Cafeteria-104
Free Glassware and Towels--137
Fury-22
Gift from the Orient—Joannie Moses-146
Go Go Boots-43
Going Downtown with My Sister-83
Gold Bond Stamps & Green Stamps-136-137
Grant's, W.T.-111
Growing up in the Sixties-29
Hairdos from 1967-57
Hats and Hankies-64-66
History of Downtown Stores-84
Hit Parade 1950s: From Pop to Rock-124
Holly Bell-94
Hot Pants-43
Housedresses-59
How Cracker Jack Began-140
How to Create a French Roll-53
Jump Rope Rhymes-7

Junior High-30 & 121
Kids' Shows-19
Kresges S. S.-110
Land of 1000 Dances, Hand Jive, Stroll-127
Lane Cedar Chests-145
Lassie-26
Long TimeGathering Spot Fountain Tea Room-87
Madras-41
Many Loves of Dobie Gillis-24
Melmac Dishes-151
Memories of Christmases Past—Betty Kieley-159
Memories Downtown/ Forum-Betty Kieley-106
Memories S&H Green Stamps/Pam Albinson-137
Mohair Sweaters-44
Muscle Cars of the 1960s & Hot Rod Fever-162
Music and Local Bands of the Sixties-127
My Best Friend and First Crush-12
My Bride Doll-10
My Hair-51
My Little Margie-25
My Love for Music-119
My Love for Paper Dolls & the Lennon Sisters--8
My Own Memories of the Nankin-104
My School Memories-4
Nankin Restaurant-102
Newspaper Patterns-39
Northern Girls-141
Pajama Parties-145
Paper Dolls--8
Patrol Picnic-119
Penney's, J. C. Downtown store-96
PennyCandy BrownPaper Sack/Linda Petroske-13
Pet Department at Woolworth's-114
Photo Machines-115

Pontiac GTO-163
Pop-it-Beads-143
Popular Cars of the 1950s-162
Popular Radio Stations-132
Popularity of Records-123
Porky's Drive In-79
Powers-97
Pretending to be Popcorn Box/Joannie Moses-74
Princess Phone-142
Prom was a Special Night-39
Real McCoys-25
Remember Aluminum Christmas Trees-158
Rifleman-21
Santa Bear-93
Saving for my Hope Chest-135
School Dances-120
Sewing and Home Ec-35
Sharing a Bike-11
Shirtwaist Dress, Shirtwaisted Woman-45-48
Shopping Downtown—Mary Dymanyk 105
Slam Books-147
Tank of My Own / Richard Worthing-76
Teen Board-94
Teenage Fashion in the 1950s-29
Top Songs of the 1960s-131
Transistor Radios-132
TV Westerns-20
Twin City Drive- Ins-71
Viet Nam 1969-122
Woolworth's-112
Working at the Nankin—Linda Herkenhoff-103
Young Quinlan-85

About the Author

At a family gathering my brother made a comment about how I've had about 75 jobs. Someone else calls out they're sure it's over a hundred. They mean no harm; they just like to tease me. It wasn't that I couldn't keep a job; I just couldn't find a job that was important enough for me to keep.

I spent many years in retail and waitressing. I also had bank and office jobs. I started out as a car hop at the Calhoun Drive-In back when I was 15. Later I worked at the school library, the sporting goods department at Fleet Farm and Target, twice.

I worked at the Nankin for one week as a busgirl and left after a waitress accused me of stealing her tips. At the Sifo Toy Company I spent more money on wooden toys than I made. I got a college scholarship and started my hair on fire at the Burger King. I got in trouble at Bridgeman's for making the turtle sundaes too big, even though my trainer taught me to make them that way. I got fired for swearing at a deaf person at Speedy Video, (a total misunderstanding). At Fanny Farmer Candy Factory I couldn't keep up with the assembly line just like Lucy and Ethel and went home with cuts on my fingers from the brown pleated papers we were supposed to fit in the box. We could eat all the turtles we wanted if they were too big; but how much chocolate can you eat? The culmination of this job was when I swore at a Russian lady in Polish (I swear I didn't know what the words meant).

I left my last job as a picture framer at Old America Store in 1993. I told my boss and my co workers I was going to write a book. They said, "Sure you are." But lo and behold four years later my first book was published. I started out writing about my one hundred jobs and of course, other topics too. So you see I finally found a job worth keeping.